The Babylonian Legends of the Creation

Sir E. A. Wallis Budge

The Babylonian Legends of the Creation

Copyright © 2023 Bibliotech Press
All rights reserved

The present edition is a reproduction of previous publication of this classic work. Minor typographical errors may have been corrected without note; however, for an authentic reading experience the spelling, punctuation, and capitalization have been retained from the original text.

ISBN: 979-8-88830-132-6

CONTENTS

CONTENTS

THE BABYLONIAN LEGENDS OF THE CREATION

AND THE

FIGHT BETWEEN BEL AND THE DRAGON

TOLD BY ASSYRIAN TABLETS FROM NINEVEH

DISCOVERY OF THE TABLETS

The baked clay tablets and portions of tablets which describe the views and beliefs of the Babylonians and Assyrians about the Creation were discovered by Mr. (later Sir) A.H. Layard, Mormuzd Rassam and George Smith, Assistant in the Department of Oriental Antiquities in the British Museum. They were found among the ruins of the Palace and Library of Ashur-bani-pal (B.C. 668-626) at Ḳuyûnjiḳ (Nineveh), between the years 1848 and 1876. Between 1866 and 1870, the great "find" of tablets and fragments, some 20,000 in number, which Rassam made in 1852, was worked through by George Smith, who identified many of the historical inscriptions of Shalmaneser II, Tiglath-Pileser III, Sargon II, Sennacherib, Esarhaddon, and other kings mentioned in the Bible, and several literary compositions of a legendary character, fables, etc. In the course of this work he discovered fragments of various versions of the Babylonian Legend of the Deluge, and portions of several texts belonging to a work which treated of the beginning of things, and of the Creation. In 1870, Rawlinson and Smith noted allusions to the Creation in the important tablet K.63, but the texts of portions of tablets of the Creation Series at that time available for study were so fragmentary that it was impossible for these scholars to find their correct sequence. During the excavations which Smith carried out at Ḳuyûnjiḳ in 1873 and 1874 for the proprietors of the *Daily Telegraph* and the Trustees of the British Museum, he was, he tells us, fortunate enough to discover "several fragments of the Genesis Legends." In January, 1875, he made an exhaustive search

1

among the tablets in the British Museum, and in the following March he published, in the *Daily Telegraph* (March 4th), a summary of the contents of about twenty fragments of the series of tablets describing the creation of the heavens and the earth. In November of the same year he communicated to the Society of Biblical Archaeology[1] copies of:—(1) the texts on fragments of the First and Fifth Tablets of Creation; (2) a text describing the fight between the "Gods and Chaos"; and (3) a fragmentary text which, he believed, described the Fall of Man. In the following year he published translations of all the known fragments of the Babylonian Creation Legends in his "Chaldean Account of Genesis" (London, 1876, 8vo, with photographs). In this volume were included translations of the Exploits of Gizdubar (Gilgamish), and some early Babylonian fables and legends of the gods.

PUBLICATION OF THE CREATION TABLETS

The publication of the above-mentioned texts and translations proved beyond all doubt the correctness of Rawlinson's assertion made in 1865, that "certain portions of the Babylonian and Assyrian Legends of the Creation resembled passages in the early chapters of the Book of Genesis." During the next twenty years, the Creation texts were copied and recopied by many Assyriologists, but no publication appeared in which all the material available for reconstructing the Legend was given in a collected form. In 1898, the Trustees of the British Museum ordered the publication of all the Creation texts contained in the Babylonian and Assyrian Collections, and the late Mr. L. W. King, Assistant in the Department of Egyptian and Assyrian Antiquities, was directed to prepare an edition. The exhaustive preparatory search which he made through the collections of tablets in the British Museum resulted in the discovery of many unpublished fragments of the Creation Legends, and in the identification of a fragment which, although used by George Smith, had been lost sight of for about twenty-five years. He ascertained also that, according to the Ninevite scribes, the Tablets of the Creation Series were seven in number, and what several versions of the Legend of the Creation,

---

[1] See the Transactions, Vol. IV, Plates I-VI, London, 1876.

2

the works of Babylonian and Assyrian editors of different periods, must have existed in early Mesopotamian Libraries. King's edition of the Creation Texts appeared in "Cuneiform Texts from Babylonian Tablets in the British Museum," Part XIII, London, 1901. As the scope of this work did not permit the inclusion of his translations, and commentary and notes, he published these in a private work entitled, "The Seven Tablets of Creation, or the Babylonian and Assyrian Legends concerning the creation of the world and of mankind," London, 1902, 8vo. A supplementary volume contained much new material which had been found by him since the appearance of the official edition of the texts, and in fact doubled the number of Creation Texts known hitherto.

Babylonian map of the world, showing the ocean surrounding the world and making the position of Babylon on the Euphrates as its centre. It shows also the mountains as the source of the river, the land of Assyria, Bît-Iakinu, and the swamps at the mouth of the Euphrates. [No. 92,687.]

THE OBJECT OF THE BABYLONIAN LEGEND
OF THE CREATION

A perusal of the texts of the Seven Tablets of Creation, which King was enabled, through the information contained in them, to arrange for the first time in their proper sequence, shows that the main object of the Legend was the glorification of the god Marduk, the son of Ea (Enki), as the conqueror of the dragon Tiâmat, and not the narration of the story of the creation of the heavens, and earth and man. The Creation properly speaking, is only mentioned as an exploit of Marduk in the Sixth Tablet, and the Seventh Tablet is devoted wholly to the enumeration of the honorific titles of Marduk. It is probable that every great city in Babylonia, whilst accepting the general form of the Creation Legend, made the greatest of its local gods the hero of it. It has long been surmised that the prominence of Marduk in the Legend was due to the political importance of the city of Babylon. And we now know from the fragments of tablets which have been excavated in recent years by German Assyriologists at Ḳal'at Sharḳât (or Shargat, or Shar'at), that in the city of Ashur, the god Ashur, the national god of Assyria, actually occupied in texts[2] of the Legend in use there the position which Marduk held in four of the Legends current in Babylonia. There is reason for thinking that the original hero of the Legend was Enlil (Bel), the great god of Nippur (the Nafar, or Nufar of the Arab writers), and that when Babylon rose into power under the First Dynasty (about B.C. 2300), his position in the Legend was usurped at Babylon by Marduk.

---

[2] See the duplicate fragments described in the Index to Ebeling, Keilschrifttexte aus Assur, Leipzig, 1919 fol.

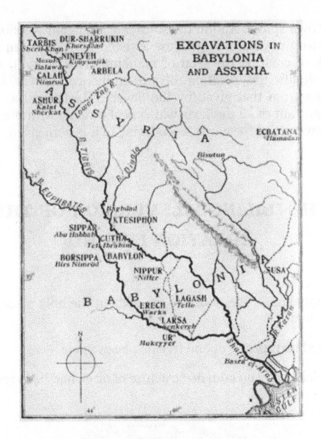

Excavations in Babylonia and Assyria

VARIANT FORMS OF THE BABYLONIAN
LEGEND OF THE CREATION

The views about the Creation which are described in the Seven Tablets mentioned above were not the only ones current in Mesopotamia, and certainly they were not necessarily the most orthodox. Though in the version of the Legend already referred to the great god of creation was Enlil, or Marduk, or Ashur, we know that in the Legend of Gilgamish (Second Tablet) it was the goddess Aruru who created Enkidu (Eabani) from a piece of clay moistened

5

with her own spittle. And in the so-called "bilingual" version[3] of the Legend, we find that this goddess assisted Marduk as an equal in the work of creating the seed of mankind. This version, although Marduk holds the position of pre-eminence, differs in many particulars from that given by the Seven Tablets, and as it is the most important of all the texts which deal directly with the creation of the heavens and the earth, a rendering of it is here given.

THE "BILINGUAL" VERSION OF THE CREATION LEGEND

1. "The holy house, the house of the gods in the holy place had not yet been made.

2. "No reed had sprung up, no tree had been made.

3. "No brick had been laid, no structure of brick had been erected.

The Bilingual Version of the Creation Legend. [No. 93,014.]

---

[3] The text is found on a tablet from Abû Habbah, Brit. Mus., No. 93,014 (82-5-22, 1048).

4. "No house had been made, no city had been built.

5. "No city had been made, no creature had been constituted.

6. "Enlil's city, [cuneiform] (i.e., Nippur) had not been made, E-kur [cuneiform] had not been built,

7. "Erech [cuneiform] had not been made, E-Aena [cuneiform] had not been built,

8. The Deep[4] (or Abyss) had not been made, Eridu [cuneiform] had not been built.">

9. "Of the holy house, the house of the gods, the dwelling-place had not been made.

10. "All the lands were sea

11. "At the time that the mid-most sea was [shaped like] a trough,

12. "At that time Eridu was made, and E-sagil was built,

13. "The E-sagil where in the midst of the Deep the god Lugal-dul-azaga[5] dwelleth,

14. "Babylon was made, E-sagil was completed.

15. "The gods the Anunnaki he created at one time.

16. "They proclaimed supreme the holy city, the dwelling of their heart's happiness.

17. "Marduk laid a rush mat upon the face of the waters,

18. "He mixed up earth and moulded it upon the rush mat,

19. "To enable the gods to dwell in the place where they fain would be.

20. "He fashioned man.

---

4 APSÛ. It is doubtful if APSÛ here really means the great abyss of waters from out of which the world was called. It was, more probably, a ceremonial object used in the cult of the god, something like the great basin, or "sea," in the court of the temple of King Solomon, mentioned in I Kings, vii, 23; 2 Kings, xxv, 13, etc.
5 This is a name under which Marduk was worshipped at Eridu.

21. "The goddess Aruru ⟨cuneiform⟩ with him created the seed of mankind.

22. "He created the beasts of the field and [all] the living things in the field.

23. "He created the river Idiglat (Tigris) and the river Purattu (Euphrates), and he set them in their places,

24. "He proclaimed their names rightly.

Terra-cotta figure of a god. From a foundation deposit at Babylon.
[No. 90,9961]

25. "He created grass, the vegetation of the marsh, seed and shrub;

26. "He created the green plants of the plain,

27. "Lands, marshes, swamps,

8

28. "The wild cow and the calf she carried, the wild calf, the sheep and the young she carried, the lamb of the fold,

29. "Plantations and shrub land,

30. "The he-goat and the mountain goat ...

31. "The lord Marduk piled up a dam in the region of the sea (*i.e.*, he reclaimed land)

32. "He ... a swamp, he founded a marsh.

33. "... he made to be

34. "Reeds he created, trees he created,

35. "... in place he created

36. "He laid bricks, he built a brick-work,

37. "He constructed houses, he formed cities.

38. "He constructed cities, creatures he set [therein].

39. "Nippur he made, E-Kur he built.

40. "[Erech he made, E-Anna] he built.

[The remainder of the text is fragmentary, and shows that the text formed part of an incantation which was recited in the Temple of E-Zida, possibly the great temple of Nabu at Borsippa.]

Bronze figure of a Babylonian god. [No. 91,147]

THE LEGEND OF THE CREATION
ACCORDING TO BEROSUS AND DAMASCIUS

Versions in Greek of the Legends found by George Smith had long been known to classical scholars, owing to the preservation of fragments of them in the works of later Greek writers, *e.g.*, Eusebius, Syncellus, and others. The most important of these is derived from the History of Babylonia, which was written in Greek by BEROSUS, a priest of Bel-Marduk, *i.e.*, the "Lord Marduk," at Babylon, about 250 B.C. In this work Berosus reproduced all the known historical facts and traditions derived from native sources which were current in his day. It is therefore not surprising to find that his account of the Babylonian beliefs about the origin of things corresponds very closely with that given in the cuneiform texts, and that it is of the greatest use in explaining and partly in expanding these texts. His account of the primeval abyss, out of which everything came, and of its inhabitants reads:—

Babylonian Monster. [No. 108,979.]

"There was a time in which there existed nothing but darkness and an abyss of waters, wherein resided most hideous beings, which were produced on a two-fold principle. There appeared men, some of whom were furnished with two wings, others with four, and with two faces. They had one body but two heads; the one that of a man, the other of a woman; and likewise in their several organs both male and female. Other human figures were to be seen with the legs and horns of goats; some had horses' feet; while others united the hind-quarters of a horse with the body of a man, resembling in shape the hippo-centaurs. Bulls likewise were bred there with the heads of men, and dogs with four told bodies, terminated in their extremities with the tails of fishes; horses also with the heads of dogs; men too and other animals, with the heads and bodies of horses and the tails of fishes. In short, there were creatures in which were combined the limbs of every species of animals. In addition to these, fishes, reptiles, serpents, with other monstrous animals, which assumed each other's shape and countenance. Of all which were preserved delineations in the temple of Belus at Babylon."

Babylonian Demon. [No. 93,089.]

[THE SLAUGHTER OF THE QUEEN OF THE ABYSS]

"The person, who presided over them, was a woman named OMUROCA; which in the Chaldean language is THALATTH; in Greek THALASSA, the sea; but which might equally be interpreted the Moon. All things being in this situation, Belus came, and cut the woman asunder: and of one half of her he formed the earth, and of the other half the heavens; and at the same time destroyed the animals within her. All this (he says) was an allegorical description of nature."

[THE CREATION OF MAN]

"For, the whole universe consisting of moisture, and animals being generated therein, the deity above-mentioned[6] took off his own head: upon which the other gods mixed the blood, as it gushed out, with the earth; and from whence were formed men. On this account it is that they are rational and partake of divine knowledge."

[BELUS CREATES THE UNIVERSE]

"This Belus, by whom they signify Jupiter, divided the darkness, and separated the Heavens from the Earth, and reduced the universe to order. But the animals not being able to bear the prevalence of light, died. Belus upon this, seeing a vast space unoccupied, though by nature fruitful, commanded one[7] of the gods to take off his head, and to mix the blood with the earth; and from thence to form other men and animals, which should be capable of bearing the air. Belus formed also the stars, and the sun, and the moon, and the five planets. Such, according to Polyhistor Alexander, is the account which Berosus gives in his first book." (See Cory, *Ancient Fragments*, London, 1832, pp. 24-26.)

In the sixth century of our era DAMASCIUS the SYRIAN, the last of the Neo-Platonic philosophers, wrote in Greek in a work on the Doubts and Solutions of the first Principles, in which he says: "But

---

[6] The god whose head was taken off was not Belus, as is commonly thought, but the god who the cuneiform texts tell us was called "Kingu."
[7] The god whose head was taken off was not Belus, as is commonly thought, but the god who the cuneiform texts tell us was called "Kingu."

the Babylonians, like the rest of the Barbarians, pass over in silence the One principle of the Universe, and they conceive Two, TAUTHE and APASON; making APASON the husband of TAUTHE, and denominating her the mother of the gods. And from these proceeds an only-begotten son, MOYMIS, which I conceive is no other than the Intelligible World proceeding from the two principles. From these, also, another progeny is derived, DACHE and DACHUS; and again, a third, KISSARE and ASSORUS, from which last three others proceed, ANUS, and ILLINUS, and AUS. And of AUS and DAUCE is born a son called Belus, who, they say, is the fabricator of the world, the Demiurgus." (See Cory, *Ancient Fragments*, London, 1832, p. 318.)

THE SEVEN TABLETS OF CREATION
DESCRIPTION OF THEIR CONTENTS

In the beginning nothing whatever existed except APSÛ, which may be described as a boundless, confused and disordered mass of watery matter; how it came into being is unknown. Out of this mass there were evolved two orders of beings, namely, demons and gods. The demons had hideous forms, even as Berosus said, which were part animal, part bird, part reptile and part human. The gods had wholly human forms, and they represented the three layers of the comprehensible world, that is to say, heaven or the sky, the atmosphere, and the underworld. The atmosphere and the underworld together formed the earth as opposed to the sky or heaven. The texts say that the first two gods to be created were LAKHMU ⟶⊦ ⊨⫼⟨ ⫞ and LAKHAMU ⟶⊦ ⫤⫼⟨ ⫞. Their attributes cannot at present be described, but they seem to represent two forms of primitive matter. They appear to have had no existence in popular religion, and it has been thought that they may be described as theological conceptions containing the notions of matter and some of its attributes.

After countless aeons had passed the gods ANSHAR ⟶⊦ ◁ and KISHAR ⟶⊦ ⟨⫤ ◁ came into being; the former represents the "hosts of heaven," and the latter the "hosts of earth."

Terra-cotta figure of a Babylonian Demon. [No. 22,458.]

After another long and indefinite period the independent gods of the Babylonian pantheon came into being, *e.g.*, ANU ⸢⸣ 𒀭 ⸢⸣, EA ⸢⸣ 𒂊 𒀭, who is here called NUDIMMUD ⸢⸣ ⸢⸣ 𒈪 ⸢⸣, and others.

Bronze figure of a Babylonian Demon. [No. 93,078.]

As soon as the gods appeared in the universe "order" came into being. When APSÛ, the personification of confusion and disorder of every kind, saw this "order," he took counsel with his female associate TIÂMAT 𒀭 𒋾 with the object of finding some means of destroying the "way" (al-ka-at) or "order" of the gods. Fortunately the Babylonians and Assyrians have supplied us with representations of Tiâmat, and these show us what form ancient tradition assigned to her. She is depicted as a ferocious monster with wings and scales and terrible claws, and her body is sometimes that of a huge serpent, and sometimes that of an animal. In the popular imagination she represented all that was physically terrifying, and foul, and abominable; she was nevertheless the mother of everything,[8] and was the possessor of the DUP SHIMATI or "TABLET OF DESTINIES" . No description of this Tablet or its contents is available, but from its name we may assume that it was a sort of Babylonian Book of Fate.[9] Theologically, Tiâmat represented to the Babylonians the same state in the development of the universe as did *tôhû wâ-bhôhû* (Genesis i. 2), *i.e.*, formlessness and voidness, of primeval matter, to the Hebrews She is depicted both on bas-reliefs and on cylinder seals in a form which associates her with LABARTU,[10] a female devil that prowled about the desert at night suckling wild animals but killing men. And it is tolerably certain that she was the type, and symbol, and head of the whole community of fiends, demons and devils.

In the consultation which took place between APSÛ and TIÂMAT, their messenger MU-UM-MU took part; of the history and attributes of this last-named god nothing is known. The result of the consultation was that a long struggle began between the demons and the gods, and it is clear that the object of the powers of darkness was to destroy the light. The whole story of this struggle is the subject of the Seven Tablets of Creation. The gods are deifications of the sun, moon, planets and other stars, and APSÛ, or CHAOS, and his companions the demons, are personifications of darkness, night and evil. The story of the fight between them is nothing more nor less than a picturesque allegory of natural phenomena. Similar descriptions are found in the literatures of

---

[8] *Muallidat gimrishun* .

[9] It is probable that the idea of this Tablet is perpetuated in the "Preserved Tablet" of the Kur'ân (Surah x, 62), on which the destiny of every man was written at or before the creation of the world. Nothing that is written (maktûb) there can be erased, or altered, or fail to take effect.

[10] (*Cun. Texts*, Part XXIV, Plate 44, l. 142).

15

other primitive nations, and the story of the great fight between Her-ur, the great god of heaven, and Set, the great captain of the hosts of darkness, may be quoted as an example. Set regarded the "order" which Ḥer-ur was bringing into the universe with the same dislike as that with which APSÛ contemplated the beneficent work of Sin, the Moon-god, Shamash, the Sun-god, and their brother gods. And the hostility of Set and his allies to the gods, like that of Tiâmat and her allies, was everlasting.

Terra-cotta plaque with a Typhonic animal in relief. [No. 103,381.]

At this point a new Text fills a break in the First Tablet, and describes the fight which took place between Nudimmud or Ea, (the representative of the established "order" which the rule of the gods had introduced into the domain of Apsû and Tiâmat) and Apsû and his envoy Mummu. Ea went forth to fight the powers of darkness and he conquered Apsû and Mummu. The victory over Apsû, *i.e.,*

16

the confused and boundless mass of primeval water, represents the setting of impassable boundaries to the waters that are on and under the earth, *i.e.*, the formation of the Ocean. The exact details of the conquest cannot be given, but we know that Ea was the possessor of the "pure (or white, or holy) incantation" and that he overcame Apsû and his envoy by the utterance of a powerful spell. In the Egyptian Legend of Rā and Āapep, the monster is rendered spell-bound by the god Ḥer-Ṭuati, who plays in it exactly the same part as Ea in the Babylonian Legend.

between Marduk (Bel) and the Dragon. Drawn from a bas-relief from the Palace of Ashur-nasir-pal, King of Assyria, 885-860 B.C., at Nimrûd. [Nimrûd Gallery, Nos. 28 and 29.]

When Tiâmat heard of Ea's victory over Apsû and Mummu she was filled with fury, and determined to avenge the death of Apsû, her husband.

The first act of TIÂMAT after the death of Apsû was to increase the number of her allies. We know that a certain creature called "UMMU-KHUBUR" at once spawned a brood of devilish monsters to help her in her fight against the gods. Nothing is known of the origin or attributes of UMMU-KHUBUR, but some think she was a form of TIÂMAT. Her brood probably consisted of personifications of mist, fog, cloud, storm, whirlwinds and the blighting and destroying powers which primitive man associated with the desert. An exact parallel of this brood of devils is found in Egyptian mythology where the allies of Set and Aāpep are called "Mesu beṭshet" *i.e.*, "spawn of impotent revolt." They are depicted in the form of serpents, and some of them became the "Nine Worms of Amenti" that are mentioned in the Book of the Dead (Chap. I*a*).

Not content with Ummu-Khubur's brood of devils, Tiâmat called the stars and powers of the air to her aid, for she "set up" (1) the Viper, (2) the Snake, (3) the god Lakhamu, (4) the Whirlwind, (5) the ravening Dog, (6) the Scorpion-man, (7) the mighty Storm-wind, (8) the Fish-man, and (9) the Horned Beast. These bore (10) the "merciless, invincible weapon," and were under the command of (11) Kingu, whom Tiâmat calls "her husband." Thus Tiâmat had Eleven mighty Helpers besides the devils spawned by Ummu-Khubur. We may note in passing that some of the above-mentioned Helpers appear among the Twelve Signs of the Zodiac which Marduk "set up" after his conquest of Tiâmat, *e.g.*, the Scorpion-man, the Horned Beast, etc. This fact suggests that the first Zodiac was "set up" by Tiâmat, who with her Eleven Helpers formed the Twelve Signs; the association of evil with certain stars may date from that period. That the Babylonians regarded the primitive gods as powers of evil is clear from the fact that Lakhamu, one of them, is enumerated among the allies of Tiâmat.

The helpers of Tiâmat were placed by her under the command of a god called KINGU who is TAMMUZ. He was the counterpart, or equivalent, of ANU, the Sky-god, in the kingdom of darkness, for it is said in the text "Kingu was exalted and received the power of Anu," *i.e.*, he possessed the same power and attributes as Anu. When Tiâmat appointed Kingu to be her captain, she recited over him a certain spell or incantation, and then she gave him the TABLET OF DESTINIES and fastened it to his breast, saying, "Whatsoever goeth forth from thy mouth shall be established." Armed with all the magical powers conferred upon him by this Tablet, and heartened by all the laudatory epithets which his wife Tiâmat heaped upon him, Kingu went forth at the head of his devils.

When Ea heard that Tiâmat had collected her forces and Was determined to continue the fight against the gods which Apsû and Mummu had begun, and that she had made her husband Kingu her champion, he was "afflicted" and "sat in sorrow." He felt unable to renew the fight against the powers of darkness, and he therefore went and reported the new happenings to Anshar, representative of the "host of heaven," and took counsel with him. When Anshar heard the matter he was greatly disturbed in mind and bit his lips, for he saw that the real difficulty was to find a worthy antagonist for Kingu and Tiâmat. A gap in the text here prevents us from knowing exactly what Anshar said and did, but the context suggests that he summoned Anu, the Sky-god, to his assistance. Then, having given him certain instructions, he sent him on an embassy to Tiâmat with the view of conciliating her. When Anu reached the place where she was he found her in a very wrathful state, and she was muttering angrily; Anu was so appalled at the sight of her that he turned and fled. It is impossible at present to explain this interlude, or to find any parallel to it in other ancient Oriental literature.

Shamash the Sun-god rising on the horizon, flames of fire ascending from his shoulder. The two portals of the dawn, each surmounted by a lion, are being drawn open by attendant gods. From a Babylonian seal cylinder in the British Museum. [No.89,110.]

When Anu reported his inability to deal with Tiâmat, a council of the gods was called, and Ea induced his son, Marduk to be present. We next find Anshar in converse with the god Marduk, who offers to act as the champion of the gods and to fight Tiâmat and her allies. Marduk being a form of the Sun-god, the greatest of all the powers of light, thus becomes naturally the protagonist of the gods, and the adversary of Tiâmat and her powers of darkness. Then Anshar

19

summoned a great council of the gods, who forthwith met in a place called "Upshukkinaku" 𒆠 𒂗 𒆠, which may be described as the Babylonian Olympus. It was all-important for Marduk to appear at the council of the gods before he undertook his task, because it was necessary for him to be formally recognised by them as their champion, and he needed to be endowed by them with magical powers. The primitive gods Lakhmu and Lakhamu, and the Igigi 𒀭 𒌋 𒈨 (or 𒀭 𒂍 𒈨 𒈨), who may be regarded as star-gods, were also summoned. A banquet was prepared, and the gods attended, and having met and kissed each other they sat down, and ate bread and drank hot and sweet sesame wine. The fumes of the wine confused their senses, but they continued to drink, and at length "their spirits were exalted." They appointed Marduk to be their champion officially, and then they proceeded to invest him with the power that would cause every command he spake to be followed immediately by the effect which he intended it to produce. Next Marduk, with the view of testing the new power which had been given him, commanded a garment to disappear and it did so; and when he commanded it to reappear it did so.

Shamash the Sun-god setting (?) on the horizon. In his right he holds a tree (?), and in his left a ... with a serrated edge. Above the horizon is a goddess who holds in her left hand an ear of corn. On the right is a god who seems to be setting free a bird from his right hand. Round him is a river with fish in it, and behind him is an attendant god; under his foot is a young bull. To the right of the goddess stand a hunting god, with a bow and lasso, and a lion. From the seal-cylinder of Adda ..., in the British Museum. About 2500 B.C. [No. 89,115.]

Then the gods saluted him as their king, and gave him the ⸻ ⸻
of royalty, namely, the sceptre, the throne and the *pala*,   ,
whatever that may be. And as they handed to him these things they
commanded him to go and hack the body of Tiâmat in pieces, and to
scatter her blood to the winds. Thereupon Marduk began to arm
himself for the fight. He took a bow, a spear, and a club; he filled his
body full of fire and set the lightning before him. He took in his
hands a net wherewith to catch Tiâmat, and he placed the four
winds near it, to prevent her from escaping from it when he had
snared her. He created mighty winds and tempests to assist him,
and grasped the thunderbolt in his hand; and then, mounting upon
the Storm, which was drawn by four horses, he went out to meet
and defeat Tiâmat. It seems pretty certain that this description of
the equipment of Marduk was taken over from a very ancient
account of the Fight with Tiâmat in which the hero was Enlil, *i.e.*,
the god of the air, or of the region which lies between heaven and
hell. Marduk approached and looked upon the "Middle" or "Inside"
or "Womb" of Tiâmat[11] ⸻ ⸻ ⸻ ⸻ ⸻ ⸻, and divined the plan
of Kingu who had taken up his place therein. In the Seventh Tablet
(l. 108) Marduk is said to have "entered into the middle of Tiâmat,"
and because he did so he is called "Nibiru," *i.e.*, "he who entered in,"
and the "seizer of the middle." What the words "middle of Tiâmat"
meant to the Babylonian we are not told, but it is clear that
Marduk's entry into it was a signal mark of the triumph of the god.
When Kingu from the "middle of Tiâmat" saw Marduk arrayed in
his terrible panoply of war, he was terrified and trembled, and
staggered about and lost all control of his legs; and at the mere sight
of the god all the other fiends and devils were smitten with fear and
reduced to helplessness. Tiâmat saw Marduk and began to revile
him, and when he challenged her to battle she flew into a rage and
attempted to overthrow him by reciting an incantation, thinking
that her words of power would destroy his strength. Her spell had
no effect on the god, who at once cast his net over her. At the same
moment he made a gale of foul wind to blow on her face, and
entering through her mouth it filled her body; whilst her body was
distended he drove his spear into her, and Tiâmat split asunder, and
her womb fell out from it. Marduk leaped upon her body and looked

---

[11] Or perhaps the "belly of Tiâmat." The Egyptians distinguished a portion
of the heavens by the name of "Khat Nut," "the belly of Nut," ⸻ ⸻
and two drawings of it are extant. The first shows an oval object rimmed
with stars and the other a pear-shaped object, with a god inside it. (See
Brugsch, *Inschriften (Astronomische)* Leipzig, 1883, p, 146.)

on her followers as they attempted to escape. But the Four Winds which he had stationed round about Tiâmat made all their efforts to flee of no effect. Marduk caught all the Eleven allies of Tiâmat in his net, and he trampled upon them as they lay in it helpless. Marduk then took the TABLET OF DESTINIES from Kingu's breast, and sealed it with his seal and placed it on his own breast.

Then returning to the dead body of Tiâmat he smashed her skull with his club and scattered her blood to the north wind, and as a reward for his destruction of their terrible foe, he received gifts and presents from the gods his fathers.

The text then goes on to say that Marduk "devised a cunning plan," *i.e.*, he determined to carry out a series of works of creation. He split the body of Tiâmat into two parts; out of one half he fashioned the dome of heaven, and out of the other he constructed the abode of Nudimmud, or Ea, which he placed over against Apsu, *i.e.*, the deep. He also formulated regulations concerning the maintenance of the same. By this "cunning plan" Marduk deprived the powers of darkness of the opportunity of repeating their revolt with any chance of success. Having established the framework of his new heaven and earth Marduk, acting as the celestial architect, set to work to furnish them. In the first place he founded E-Sharra ⊨⫲⫲⫲ ◁ ⊨⫲⫲, or the mansion of heaven, and next he set apart and arranged proper places for the old gods of the three realms—Anu, Bel and Ea.

Tablet sculptured with a scene representing the worship of the

22

Sun-god in the Temple of Sippar. The Sun-god is seated on a throne within a pavilion holding in one hand a disk and bar which (like Ω in Egyptian) may symbolize eternity. Above his head are the three symbols of the Moon, the Sun, and the planet Venus. On a stand in front of the pavilion rests the disk of the Sun, which is held in position by ropes grasped in the hands of two divine beings who are supported by the roof of the pavilion. The pavilion of the Sun-god stands on the Celestial Ocean, and the four small disks indicate either the four cardinal points or the tops of the pillars of the heavens. The three figures in front of the disk represent the high priest of Shamash, the king (Nabu-aplu-iddina, about 870 B.C.) and an attendant goddess. [No. 91,000.]

The text of the Fifth Tablet, which would undoubtedly have supplied details as to Marduk's arrangement and regulations for the sun, the moon, the stars, and the Signs of the Zodiac in the heavens is wanting. The prominence of the celestial bodies in the history of creation is not to be wondered at, for the greater number of the religious beliefs of the Babylonians are grouped round them. Moreover, the science of astronomy had gone hand in hand with the superstition of astrology in Mesopotamia from time immemorial; and at a very early period the oldest gods of Babylonia were associated with the heavenly bodies. Thus the Annunaki and the Igigi, who are bodies of deified spirits, were identified with the stars of the northern and southern heaven, respectively. And all the primitive goddesses coalesced and were grouped to form the goddess Ishtar, who was identified with the Evening and Morning Star, or Venus. The Babylonians believed that the will of the gods was made known to men by the motions of the planets, and that careful observation of them would enable the skilled seer to recognize in the stars favourable and unfavourable portents. Such observations, treated from a magical point of view, formed a huge mass of literature which was being added to continually. From the nature of the case this literature enshrined a very considerable number of facts of pure astronomy, and as early as the period of the First Dynasty (about 2000 B.C.), the Babylonians were able to calculate astronomical events with considerable accuracy, and to reconcile the solar and lunar years by the use of epagomenal months. They had by that time formulated the existence of the Zodiac, and fixed the "stations" of the moon, and the places of the planets with it; and they had distinguished between the planets and the fixed stars. In the Fifth Tablet of the Creation Series (l. 2) the

Signs of the Zodiac are called Lumashi,[12] but unfortunately no list of their names is given in the context. Now these are supplied by the little tablet (No. 77,821) of the Persian Period of which a reproduction is here given. It has been referred to and discussed by various scholars, and its importance is very great. The transcript of the text, which is now published (see p. 68) for the first time, will be acceptable to the students of the history of the Zodiac. Egyptian, Greek, Syriac and Arabic astrological and astronomical texts all associate with the Signs of the Zodiac twelve groups, each containing three stars, which are commonly known as the "Thirty-six Dekans."[13] The text of line 4 of the Fifth Tablet of the Creation Series proves that the Babylonians were acquainted with these groups of stars, for we read that Marduk "set up for the twelve "months of the year three stars apiece." In the List of Signs of the Zodiac here given, it will be seen that each Sign is associated with a particular month.

OBVERSE

REVERSE

Tablet inscribed with a list of the Signs of the Zodiac. [No. 77,821.]

---

[12] This is the original of the Syriac word for the Signs of the Zodiac malwâshê (plural of malwâshâ). The Syrians added to it an m, thus giving it a participial form.

[13] Δεκανοί also called πρόσωπα, ὡροσκόποι, φύλακες and ἐπίσκοποι. They were well known to the Egyptians, who, as early as the fourteenth century B.C., possessed a full list of them. See Lepsius, Chronologie, Berlin, 1848, and Brugsch, Thesaurus (Astronomische und Astrologische Inschriften), Leipzig, 1883.

At a later period, say about 500 B.C., the Babylonians made some of the gods regents of groups of stars, for Enlil ruled 33 stars, Anu 23 stars, and Ea 15 stars. They also possessed lists of the fixed stars, and drew up tables of the times of their heliacal risings. Such lists were probably based upon very ancient documents, and prove that the astral element in Babylonian religion was very considerable.

The accompanying illustration, which is reproduced from the Boundary Stone of Ritti-Marduk (Brit. Mus., No. 90,858), supplies much information about the symbols of the gods, and of the Signs of the Zodiac in the reign of Nebuchadnezzar I, King of Babylon, about 1120 B.C.. Thus in Register 1, we have the Star of Ishtar, the crescent of the Moon-god Sin, and the disk of Shamash the Sun-god. In Reg. 2 are three stands (?) surmounted by tiaras, which represent the gods Anu, Enlil (Bel) and Ea respectively. In Reg. 3 are three altars (?) or shrines (?) with a monster in Nos. 1 and 2. Over the first is the lance of Marduk, over the second the mason's square of Nabû, and over the third is the symbol of the goddess Ninkharsag, the Creatress. In Reg. 4 are a standard with an animal's head, a sign of Ea; a two-headed snake = the Twins; an unknown symbol with a horse's head, and a bird, representative of Shukamuna and Shumalia. In Reg. 5 are a seated figure of the goddess Gula and the Scorpion-man; and in Reg. 6 are forked lightning, symbol of Adad, above a bull, the Tortoise, symbol of Ea (?), the Scorpion of the goddess Ishkhara, and the Lamp of Nusku, the Fire-god. Down the left-hand side is the serpent-god representing the constellation of the Hydra.

The mutilated text of the Fifth Tablet makes it impossible to gain further details in connection with Marduk's work in arranging the heavens. We are, however, justified in assuming that the gaps in it contained statements about the grouping of the gods into triads. In royal historical inscriptions the kings often invoke the gods in threes, though they never call any one three a triad or trinity. It seems as if this arrangement of gods in threes was assumed to be of divine origin. In the Fourth Tablet of Creation, one triad "Anu-Bel-Ea" is actually mentioned, and in the Fifth Tablet, another is indicated, "Sin-Shamash-Ishtar." In these triads Anu represents the sky or heaven, Bel or Enlil the region under the sky and including the earth, Ea the underworld, Sin the Moon, Shamash the Sun, and Ishtar the star Venus. When the universe was finally constituted several other great gods existed, *e.g.*, Nusku, the Fire-god, Enurta,[14]

---

[14] Formerly known as Ninip.

a solar god, Nergal, the god of war and handicrafts, Nabu, the god of learning, Marduk of Babylon, the great national god of Babylonia, and Ashur, the great national god of Assyria.

When Marduk had arranged heaven and earth, and had established the gods in their places, the gods complained that their existence was barren, because they lacked worshippers at their shrines and offerings. To make a way out of this difficulty Marduk devised another "cunning plan," and announced his intention of creating man out of "blood and bone" DAMI IṢṢIMTUM 𒁹𒌋 𒀖 𒂊𒌋 𒀀𒈾 𒈨. We have already quoted (see p. 10) the statement of Berosus that man was created out of the blood of a god mixed with earth; here, then, is the authority for his words. Marduk made known to Ea his intention of creating man, and Ea suggested that if one of the gods were sacrificed the remainder of them should be set free from service, presumably to Marduk. Thereupon Marduk summons a council of the gods, and asks them to name the instigator of the fight in which he himself was the victor. In reply the gods named Kingu, Tiâmat's second husband, whom they seized forthwith, and bound with fetters and carried to Ea, and then having "inflicted punishment upon him they let his blood." From Kingu's blood Ea fashioned mankind for the service of the gods.

Now among the texts which have been found on the tablets at Ḳal'at Sharḳât is an account of the creation of man which differs from the version given in the Seven Tablets of Creation, but has two features in common with it. These two features are: (1) the council of the gods to discuss the creation of man; (2) the sacrifice which the gods had to make for the creation of man. In the variant version two (or more) gods are sacrificed, 𒀭 𒉺𒅗 𒀭 𒉺𒅗, *Ilu Nagar Ilu Nagar*, *i.e.*, "the workmen gods," about whom nothing is known. The place of sacrifice is specified with some care, and it is said to be "Uzu-mu-a, or the bond of heaven and earth." Uzu-mu-a may be the bolt with which Marduk locked the two halves of Tiâmat into place.

The Anunnaki, wishing to give an expression of their admiration for Marduk's heroism, decided to build him a shrine or temple. To this Marduk agreed, and chose Babylon, *i.e.*, the "Gate of God," for its site. The Anunnaki themselves made the bricks, and they built the great temple of E-Sagila at Babylon. When the temple was finished, Marduk re-enacted the scene of creation; for, as he had formerly assigned to each god his place in the heavens, so now he assigned to each god his place in E-Sagila. The tablet ends with a long hymn of praise which the Anunnaki sang to Marduk, and describes the summoning of an assembly of the gods to proclaim ceremonially the great Fifty Names of this god. Thus the gods accepted the absolute supremacy of Marduk.

27

From the above it is clear that a dispute broke out between Marduk and the gods after he had created them, and the tradition of it has made its way into the religious literatures of the Hebrews, Syrians, Arabs, Copts and Abyssinians. The cuneiform texts tell us nothing about the cause of the dispute, but tradition generally ascribes it to the creation of man by the supreme God; and it is probable that all the apocryphal stories which describe the expulsion from heaven of the angels who contended against God under the leadership of Satan, or Satnael, or Iblîs, are derived from a Babylonian original which has not yet been found. The "Fifty Names," or laudatory epithets mentioned above, find parallels in "Seventy-five Praises of Rā," sung by the Egyptians under the XIXth dynasty,[15] and in the "Ninety-nine Beautiful Names of Allâh," which are held in such great esteem by the Muḥammadans.[16] The respect in which the Fifty Names were held by the Babylonians is well shown by the work of the Epilogue on the Seventh Tablet, where it is said, "Let them be held in remembrance, let the first-comer (i.e., any and every man) proclaim them; let the wise and the understanding consider them together. Let the father repeat them and teach them to his son. Let them be in the ears of the herdsman and the shepherd."

The object of the writer of the Fifty Names was to show that Marduk was the "Lord of the gods," that the power, qualities and attributes of every god were enshrined in him, and that they all were merely forms of him. This fact is proved by the tablet (No. 47,406),[17] which contains a long list of gods who are equated with Marduk in his various forms.[18] The tendency in the later Babylonian religion to make Marduk the god above all gods has led many to think that monotheistic conceptions were already in existence among the Babylonians as early as the period of the First Dynasty, about 2000 B.C. It is indisputable that Marduk obtained his pre-eminence in the Babylonian Pantheon at this early period. But some authorities deny the existence of monotheistic conceptions among the Babylonians at that time, and attribute Marduk's kingship of the gods to the influence of the political situation of the time, when Babylon first became the capital of the country, and mistress of the greater part of

---

[15] See Naville, La Litanie du Soleil, Paris, 1875, Plate ii ff.
[16] See Kur'ân, Surah vii, v. 179. That there were ninety-nine Beautiful Names of God rests on the authority of Abû Hurairah, who repeats the statement as made by Muhammad the Prophet.
[17] Published by King, Cuneiform Texts, Part XXV, Plate 50.
[18] Thus he is equated with En-Urta, Nergal, En-lil, Nabû, Sin, Shamash, Adad, etc.

the known world. Material for deciding this question is wanting, but it may be safely said that whatever monotheistic conceptions existed at that time, their acceptance was confined entirely to the priests and scribes. They certainly find no expression in the popular religious texts.

Both the source of the original form of the Legend of the Fight between Ea and Apsu, and Marduk and Tiâmat, and the period of its composition are unknown, but there is no doubt that in one form or another it persisted in Mesopotamia for thousands of years. The apocryphal book of "Bel and the Dragon" shows that a form of the Legend was in existence among the Babylonian Jews long after the Captivity, and the narrative relating to it associates it with religious observances. But there is no foundation whatsoever for the assertion which has so often been made that the Two Accounts of the Creation which are given in the early chapters in Genesis are derived from the Seven Tablets of Creation described in the preceding pages. It is true that there are many points of resemblance between the narratives in cuneiform and Hebrew, and these often illustrate each other, but the fundamental conceptions of the Babylonian and Hebrew accounts are essentially different. In the former the earliest beings that existed were foul demons and devils, and the God of Creation only appears at a later period, but in the latter the conception of God is that of a Being Who existed in and from the beginning, Almighty and Alone, and the devils of chaos and evil are His servants.

Marduk destroying Tiâmat, who is here represented in the form of a huge serpent. From a seal-cylinder in the British Museum. [No. 89,589.]

Among the primitive Semitic peoples there were probably many versions of the story of the Creation; and the narrative told by the Seven Tablets is, no doubt, one of them in a comparatively modern form. It is quite clear that the Account of the Creation given in the Seven Tablets is derived from very ancient sources, and a considerable amount of literary evidence is now available for reconstructing the history of the Legend. Thus in the Sumerian Account the narrative of the exploits of the hero called ZIUSUDU[19] ⊢⫫⊰ ⊣⫪ ⊱⊢ ⊢⊣⫪begins with a description of the Creation and then goes on to describe a Flood, and there is little doubt that certain passages in this text are the originals of the Babylonian version as given in the Seven Tablets. In the Story of ZIUSUDU, however, there is no mention of any Dragon. And there is reason to think that the Legend of the Dragon had originally nothing whatever to do with the Creation, for the texts of fragments of two distinct Accounts[20] of the Creation describe a fight between a Dragon and some deity other than Marduk. In other Accounts the Dragon bears a strong resemblance to the Leviathan of Psalm civ, 26; Job xli, 1. In the one text he is said to be 50 *biru*[21] in length, and 1 *biru* in thickness; his mouth was 6 cubits (about 9 feet) wide, and the circumference of his ears 12 cubits (18 feet). He was slain by a god whose name is unknown, and the blood continued to flow from his body for three years, three months, one day and one night. In the second text the Dragon is 60 *biru* long and his thickness is 30 *biru*; the diameter of each eye is half a *biru*, and his paws are 20 *biru* long. Thus there is every reason for believing that the Legend as it is given in the Seven Tablets is the work of some editor, who added the Legend of the Creation to the Legend of the Dragon in much the same way as the editor of the Gilgamish Legends included an account of the Deluge in his narrative of the exploits of his hero. All forms of the Legend of the Creation and of the Dragon were popular in Babylonia, and one of them achieved so much notoriety that the priest employed recited it as an incantation to charm away the toothache.

The literary form of the text of the Seven Tablets fulfils the requirements of Semitic poetry in general. The lines usually fall into couplets, the second line being the antiphon of the first, *e.g.*:—

---

[19] See Poebel, Historical Texts, No. 1.
[20] See King, Cuneiform Texts, Part XIII, Plate 33; and Ebellog, Assurtexte, I, No. 6.
[21] The biru was the distance which a man would travel in two hours.

"When in the height heaven was not named,
And the earth beneath did not yet bear a name."

Each line, or verse, falls into two halves, and a well-marked caesura divides each line, or verse, into two equally accented parts. And the half-lines can be further resolved into two halves, each containing a single accented word or phrase. This is proved by tablet Spartali ii, 265A, where the scribe writes his lines and spaces the words in such a way as to show the subdivision of the lines. Thus we have:—

enuma | elish || lâ nabû | shamamu
shaplish | ammatum || shuma | lâ zakrat

Here there is clearly a rhythm which resembles that found in the poems of the Syrians and Arabs, but there are many instances of its inconsistent use in several parts of the text. Both rhyme and alliteration appear to be used occasionally.

THE SEVEN TABLETS OF CREATION— TRANSLATION

FIRST TABLET[22]

1. When the heavens above were yet unnamed,[23]

2. And the name of the earth beneath had not been recorded,

3. Apsu, the oldest of beings, their progenitor,

4. "Mummu" Tiâmat, who bare each and all of them—

5. Their waters were merged into a single mass.

---

[22] This translation is made from transcripts of the British Museum fragments (Cuneiform Texts, Part XIII), and transcripts of the Berlin fragments (Ebeling, Keilschrifttexte aus Assur, Nos. 117, 118).

[23] The name of an object was the object itself, and it was believed that nothing could exist apart from its name.

6. A field had not been measured, a marsh had not been searched out,

7. When of the gods none was shining,

Portion of a tablet inscribed in Assyrian with a text of the First Tablet of the Creation Series. [K. 5419C.]

8. A name had not been recorded, a fate had not been fixed,

9. The gods came into being in the midst of them.

10. The god Lakhmu and the goddess Lakhamu were made to shine, they were named.

11. [Together] they increased in stature, they grew tall.

12. Anshar and Kishar came into being, and others besides them.

13. Long were the days, the years increased.

14. The god Anu, their son, the equal of his fathers, [was created].

15. The god Anshar made his eldest son Anu in his own image.

16. And the god Anu begat Nudimmud (Ea) the image of himself.

17. The god Nudimmud was the first among his fathers,

18. Endowed with understanding, he who thinketh deeply, the orator

19. Exceedingly mighty in strength above his father Anshar who begat him.

20. Unrivalled amongst the gods his brothers ...

21. The confraternity of the gods was established.

22. Tiâmat was troubled and she ... their guardian.

23. Her belly was stirred up to its uttermost depths.

24. ....

25. Apsu (the watery abyss) could not diminish their brawl

26. And Tiâmat gathered herself together ...

27. She struck a blow, and their works ...

28. Their way was not good,...

29. At that time Apsu, the progenitor of the great gods,

30. Shouted out and summoned Mummu, the steward of his house, saying

31. "[O] Mummu, my steward, who makest my liver to rejoice,

32. "Come, to Tiâmat we will go."

33. They went, they lay down [on a couch] facing Tiâmat.

34. They took counsel together about the gods [their children].

35. Apsu took up his word and said,

36. To Tiâmat, the holy (?) one, he made mention of a matter, [saying],

37. "... their way ...

38. "By day I find no peace, by night I have no rest.

39. "Verily I will make an end of their way, I will sweep them away,

40. "There shall be a sound of lamentation; lo, then we shall rest."

41. Tiâmat on hearing this

42. Was stirred up to wrath and shrieked to her husband,[24]

43. ... unto sickness. She raged all alone,

44. She uttered a curse, and unto [Apsu, spake, saying,],

45. "Whatsoever we have made we will destroy.

46. "Verily their way shall be filled with disaster; lo, then we shall rest."

47. Mummu answered and gave counsel unto Apsu,

48. The counsel of Mummu was ... and dire [in respect of the gods]:

49. "Come, [do thou destroy] their way which is strong.

50. "Then verily by day thou shalt find peace, [and] by night thou shalt have rest."

51. Apsu heard him, his face grew bright,

52. For that they were planning evil against the gods, his children.

53. Mummu embraced his neck ...

54. He took him on his knee, he kissed him ...

55. They (*i.e.* Mummu and Apsu) planned the cursing in the assembly,

56. They repeated the curses to the gods their eldest sons.

57. The gods made answer ...

58. They began a lamentation...

59. [Endowed] with understanding, the prudent god, the exalted one,

---

[24] Tiâmat's wrath was roused by Apsu, who had proposed to slay the gods, her children. She took no part in the first struggle of Apsu and Mummu against the gods, and only engaged in active hostilities to avenge Apsu.

60. Ea, who pondereth everything that is, searched out their [plan].

61. He brought it to nought (?), he made the form of everything to stand still.

62. He recited a cunning incantation, very powerful and holy.

[In the British Museum tablets lines 63-108 are either wanting entirely, or are too broken to translate, and the last 130 lines of the Berlin fragment are much mutilated. The fragments of text show that Ea waged war against Apsu and Mummu. Ea recited an incantation which caused Apsu to fall asleep. He then "loosed the joints" of Mummu, who in some way suffered, but he was strong enough to attack Ea when he turned to deal with Apsu. Ea overcame both his adversaries and divided Apsu into chambers and laid fetters upon him. In one of the chambers of Apsu a god was begotten and born. According to the Ninevite theologians Ea begat by his wife, who is not named, his son Marduk, and according to the theologians of the City of Ashur, Lakhmu begat by his wife Lakhamu a son who is no other than Anshar, or Ashur. A nurse was appointed to rear him, and he grew up a handsome child, to the great delight of his father. He had four ears and four eyes, a statement which suggests that he was two-headed, and resembled the Latin god Janus.]

109. They formed a band, and went forth to battle to help Tiâmat.

110. They were exceedingly wroth, they made plots by day and by night without ceasing.

111. They offered battle, fuming and raging.

112. They set the battle in array, they uttered cries[25] of hostility,

113. Ummu-Khubur,[26] who fashioned all things,

114. Set up the unrivalled weapon, she spawned huge serpents,

115. Sharp of tooth, pitiless in attack (?)

116. She filled their bodies with venom instead of blood,

117. Grim, monstrous serpents, arrayed in terror,

---

[25] Literally, "they excited themselves to hostility."
[26] A title of Tiâmat.

35

118. She decked them with brightness, she fashioned them in exalted forms,

119. So that fright and horror might overcome him that looked upon them,

120. So that their bodies might rear up, and no man resist their attack,

121. She set up the Viper, and the Snake, and the god Lakhamu,

122. The Whirlwind, the ravening Dog, the Scorpion-man,

123. The mighty Storm-wind, the Fish-man, the horned Beast (Capricorn?)

124. They carried the Weapon[27] which spared not, nor flinched from the battle.

125. Most mighty were Tiâmat's decrees, they could not be resisted,

126. Thus she caused eleven [monsters] of this kind to come into being,

127. Among the gods, her first-born son who had collected her company,

128. That is to say, Kingu, she set on high, she made him the great one amongst them,

129. Leader of the hosts in battle, disposer of the troops,

130. Bearer of the firmly grasped weapon, attacker in the fight,

131. He who in the battle is the master of the weapon,

132. She appointed, she made him to sit down in [goodly apparel]

133. [Saying], "I have uttered the incantation for thee. I have magnified thee in the assembly of the gods.

----

[27] These nine monsters with the Weapon (Thunderbolt?) and Kingu form the Eleven Allies of Tiâmat, and it is clear that she and her Allies represent the Twelve Signs of the Zodiac. When Marduk destroyed Tiâmat and her associates, he found it necessary to fix the stars, the images of the great gods, in their places, as the Twelve Signs of the Zodiac. (See the Fifth Tablet of Creation, p. 55.)

134. "I have filled his [*sic*, read 'thy'] hand with the sovereignty of the whole company of the gods.

135. "Mayest thou be magnified, thou who art my only spouse,

136. "May the Anunnaki make great thy renown over all of them."

137. She gave him the TABLET OF DESTINIES, she fastened it on his breast, [saying],

138. "As for thee, thy command shall not fall empty, whatsoever goeth forth from thy mouth shall be established."

139. When Kingu was raised on high and had taken the heavens (literally, the god Anutum)

140. He fixed the destinies for the gods his sons,

141. Open your mouths, let the Fire-god[28] be quenched,

142. He who is glorious in battle and is most mighty, shall do great deeds.

SECOND TABLET

1. Tiâmat made solid that which she had moulded.

2. She bound the gods her children with [evil bonds].

3. Tiâmat wrought wickedness to avenge Apsu.

4. When ... had harnessed his chariot he went to meet Ea,

5. Ea hearkened to his story,

6. He was sorely afflicted and abode in sorrow,

7. The days were long, his wrath died down.

---

[28] The god here alluded to is Mardak, who, in one aspect, is a fire-god; see Tablet IV, II. 39, 40.

8. He went his way to the dwelling of Anshar, his father,

9. He went into the presence of Anshar, the father who begat him,

Portion of a tablet inscribed in Assyrian with a text of the Second Tablet of the Creation Series. [No. 40,559.]

10. Whatsoever Tiâmat had devised he repeated unto him,

11. Mother Tiâmat who gave us birth hath sown these things.

12. She hath set in order her assembly, she rageth furiously,

13. All the gods have joined themselves to her.

14. They march by her side together with those whom ye have created.

15. They formed a band and went forth to battle to help Tiâmat,

16. They were exceedingly wroth, they made plots by day and by night without ceasing,

17. They offered battle, fuming and raging,

18. They set the battle in array, they uttered cries of defiance.

19. Ummu-Khubur,[29] who fashioned all things,

20. Set up the unrivalled weapon, she spawned huge serpents

21. Sharp of tooth, pitiless in attack (?)

22. She filled their bodies with venom instead of blood,

23. Grim, monstrous serpents arrayed in terror.

24. She decked them with brightness, she fashioned them in exalted forms,

25. So that fright and horror might overcome him that looked upon them,

26. So that their bodies might rear up, and no man resist their attack.

27. She set up the Viper, and the Snake, and the god Lakhamu,

28. The Whirlwind, the ravening Dog, the Scorpion-man,

29. The Storm-wind, the Fish-man, the Horned Beast.

30. They carried the Weapon which spared not, nor flinched from the battle.

31. Most mighty were Tiâmat's allies, they could not be resisted.

32. Thus she caused eleven [monsters] of this kind to come into being.

33. Among the gods, her first-born son who had collected her company,

34. That is to say, Kingu, she set on high, she made him the great one amongst them.

---

[29] See above.

35. Leader of the hosts in battle, disposer of the troops,

36. Bearer of the firmly-grasped weapon, attacker in the fight,

37. He who in the battle is the master of the weapon,

38. She appointed, she made him to sit down in [goodly apparel]

39. [Saying], "I have recited the incantation for thee, I have magnified thee in the assembly of the gods,

40. "I have filled his [*sic*, read 'thy'] hand with the sovereignty of the whole company of the gods.

41. "Mayest thou be magnified, thou who art my only spouse,

42. "May the Anunnaki make great thy renown over all of them."

43. She gave him the TABLET OF DESTINIES, she fastened it on his breast, [saying]—

44. "As for thee, thy command shall not fall empty, what goeth forth from thy mouth shall be established."

45. When Kingu was raised on high and had taken the heavens (literally, "the god Anutum") 46. He fixed the destinies for the gods his sons, [saying],

47. "Open your mouths, let the Fire-god be quenched,

48. "He who is glorious in battle and is most mighty shall do great deeds."

49. When Anshar heard that Tiâmat was stirred mightily,

50. ... he bit his lips

51. ... his mind was not at peace

[Lines 52-54 too fragmentary for translation.]

An'shar then addresses Ea and says:—

55. "Thou hast slain Mummu and Apsu

56. "But Tiâmat hath exalted Kingu—where is the one who can meet her?

40

[Lines 57 and 58 imperfect; lines 59-71 wanting.]

72. Anshar spake a word unto his son [Anu]:—

73. "... this is a difficulty, my warrior

74. "Whose power is exalted, whose attack cannot be stayed,

75. "Go and stand thou in the presence of Tiâmat,

76. "That her spirit [be quieted], her heart softened.

77. "But should she not hearken unto thy word,

78. "Speak thou our word unto her so that she may be abated."

79. [Anu] heard the order of his father Anshar.

80. He took the straight road to her, and hastened on the way to her.

81. Anu drew nigh, he searched out the plan of Tiâmat,

82. He could not prevail against her, he turned back.

Lines 83 and 84 contain Anu's report to Anshar, but they are too fragmentary to translate; line 85 reads:—

83. He (Anu) went to his father Anshar who begat him,

84. He spake unto him a word [concerning Tiâmat]

85. [She laid] hands upon me that withered me up."

86. Anshar was distressed, he looked down upon the ground,

87. He turned pale; towards Ea he lifted up his head.

88. All the Anunnaki assembled at their posts.

89. They shut their mouths, they sat in lamentation.

90. [They said], "Nowhere is there a god who can attack Tiâmat.

91. "He would not escape from Tiâmat's presence with his life."

92. The Lord Anshar, the Father of the gods, [spake] majestically,

41

93. He lifted up his heart, he addressed the Anunnaki, [saying]

94. "He whose [strength] is mighty [shall be] an avenger for [us]

95. "The ... in the strife, Marduk the Hero."

96. Ea called Marduk to the place where he gave oracles,

97. Marduk came and according to his heart he addressed him,

98. [Saying], "O Marduk, hear the counsel and advice of thy father,

99. "Thou art the son who refresheth his heart,

100. "Draw nigh and enter the presence of An-shar,

101. "Stand there [with joy], when he looketh upon thee he will be at rest."[30]

113. The Lord [Marduk] rejoiced at the word of his father,

114. He approached and took up his place before Anshar.

115. Anshar looked upon him and his heart was filled with gladness.

116. He (*i.e.*, Anshar) kissed his (Marduk's) lips, and his (Anshar's) fear was removed. [Then Marduk said]

117. "My father, let not the opening of thy mouth be closed,[31]

118. "I will go, I will make to take place all that is in thy heart.

119. "Anshar, let not the opening of thy mouth be closed,

120. "I will go, I will make to take place all that is in thy heart." [Anshar says to Marduk]

121. "What man is the cause of the battle which made thee go forth

122. "... Tiâmat, who is a woman, pursueth thee with weapons.

123. "Rejoice our [hearts] and make us glad.

---

[30] Lines 83, 84, 88-101 are translated from the British Museum fragments and the Berlin fragments; lines 88-101 contain the equivalent to the whole gap in the British Museum tablet.
[31] i.e., "let what thou sayest prevail."

124. "Thou thyself shalt soon trample upon the neck of Tiâmat,

125. "Rejoice our [hearts] and make us glad.

126. "Thou thyself shalt soon trample upon the neck of Tiâmat.

127. "My son, who dost comprehend everything,

128. "Cast deep sleep upon Tiâmat with thy holy spell.

129. "Betake thyself to thy march with all speed.

130. "..."

131. The Lord [Marduk] rejoiced at the word of his father,

132. His heart leaped with joy, to his father he spake, [saying],

133. "O Lord of the gods, Overlord of the Great Gods,

134. "Should I as your avenger

135. "Slay Tiâmat and bestow life upon you,

136. "Summon a meeting, proclaim and magnify my position,

137. "Sit ye down together in friendly fashion in Upshukkinaku.

138. "Let me issue decrees by the opening of my mouth even as ye do.

139. "Whatsoever I bring to pass let it remain unaltered,

140. "That which my mouth uttereth shall never fail or be brought to nought."

THIRD TABLET

1. Anshar opened his mouth, and

2. Unto the god Gaga (⸝⊦ ⊧⫶⫶⸜ ⊧⫶⫶⸜), his envoy, spake a word [saying],

3. "O Gaga, my envoy, who makest glad my liver.

4. "I will despatch thee unto the gods Lakhmu and Lakhamu.

Portion of a tablet inscribed in Assyrian with a text of the Third Tablet of the Creation Series. [No. 93,017.]

5. "Thou must know and understand the [intention of my heart]

6. "... are brought before thee

7. "... all the gods.

8. "Let them make a council, let them sit down to a feast

9. "Let them eat bread, let them heat sesame wine.

10. "Let them issue decrees to Marduk as their avenger.

11. "Get thee gone, Gaga, take up thy stand before them.

12. "All that I am now going to tell thee do thou repeat to them [saying],

13. "'[O ye gods], Anshar your son hath charged me,

14. "'The intention of his heart he hath made me to know in this wise:—

15. "'Mother Tiâmat who gave us birth hath sown these things,

16. "'She hath set in order her assembly, she rageth furiously,

17. "'All the gods have joined themselves to her.

18. "'They march by her side together with those whom ye have created.

19. "'They formed a band and went forth to battle to help Tiâmat.

20. "'They were exceedingly wroth, they made plots by day and by night without ceasing.

21. "'They offered battle, foaming and raging.

22. "'They set the battle in array, they uttered cries of defiance.

23. "'Ummu-Khubur, who formed all things,

24. "'Set up the unrivalled weapon, she spawned huge serpents,

25. "'Sharp of tooth, pitiless in attack (?)

26. "'She filled their bodies with venom instead of blood.

27. "'Grim, monstrous serpents arrayed in terror.

28. "'She decked them with brightness, she fashioned them in exalted forms,

29. "'So that fright and horror might overcome him that looked upon them,

30. "'So that their bodies might rear up, and no man resist their attack.

31. "'She set up the Viper, and the Snake, and the god Lakhamu,

32. "'The Whirlwind, the Ravening Dog, the Scorpion-man,

33. "'The Storm-wind, the Fish-man, the Horned Beast.

34. "'They carried the Weapon which spared not, nor flinched from the battle,

35. "'Most mighty were Tiâmat's allies, they could not be resisted.

36. "'Thus she caused Eleven [monsters] of this kind to come into being.

37. "'Among the gods, her first-born son who had collected her company,

38. "'That is to say, Kingu, she set on high, she made him the great one among them,

39. "'Leader of the hosts in the battle, disposer of the troops,

40. "'Bearer of the firmly-grasped weapon, attacker in the fight.

41. "'He who in the battle is the master of the weapon,

42. "'She appointed, she made him to sit down in [goodly apparel]

43. "'[Saying]: I have recited the incantation for thee, I have magnified thee in the assembly of the gods.

44. "'I have filled his (*i.e.*, thy) hand with the sovereignty of the whole company of the gods.

45. "'Mayest thou be magnified, thou who art my only spouse,

46. "'May the Anunnaki make great thy renown over all of them.'"

47. "She gave him the TABLET OF DESTINIES, she fastened it on his head [saying]:

48. "'As for thee, thy command shall not fall empty, what goeth forth from thy mouth shall be established.'

49. "When Kingu was raised on high and had taken the heavens (literally, the god Anutum),

50. "He fixed the destinies for the gods, his sons, [saying]:

46

51. "'Open your mouths, let the Fire-god be quenched.

52. "'He who is glorious in battle and is most mighty shall do great deeds.'

53. "'I sent the god Anu, but he could not prevail against her.

54. "'Nudimmud (*i.e.*, Ea) was afraid and turned back,

55. "'Marduk, your son, the envoy of the gods, hath set out.

56. "'His heart is stirred up to oppose Tiâmat.

57. "'He opened his mouth, he spoke unto me [saying]:

58. "'Should I as your avenger

59. "'Slay Tiâmat, and bestow life upon you,

60. "'Summon a meeting, proclaim and magnify my position,

61. "'Sit ye down together in friendly fashion in Up-shukkinaku.

62. "'Let me issue decrees by the opening of my mouth even as ye do,

63. "'Whatsoever I bring to pass let it remain unaltered.

64. "'That which my mouth uttereth shall neither fail nor be brought to nought.'

65. "Hasten ye therefore, issue your decrees speedily

66. "That he may go to meet your mighty enemy."

67. Gaga departed and hastened upon his way

68. To the god Lakhmu and the goddess Lakhamu, the gods his fathers, reverently

69. He did homage, and he kissed the ground at their feet.

70. He bowed down, stood up, and spake unto them [saying]:

71. "[O ye gods], Anshar your son hath charged me,

72. "The intention of his heart he hath made me to know in this wise:—

47

73. "Mother Tiâmat who gave us birth hath sown these things,

74. "She hath set in order her assembly, she rageth furiously.

75. "All the gods have joined themselves to her.

76. "They march by her side together with those whom ye have created,

77. "They formed a band and went forth to battle to help Tiâmat.

78. "They were exceedingly wroth, they made plans by day and by night without ceasing.

79. "They offered battle, foaming and raging.

80. "They set the battle in array, they uttered cries of defiance.

81. "Ummu-Khubur, who formed all things,

82. "Set up the unrivalled weapon, she spawned huge serpents,

83. "Sharp of tooth, pitiless in attack (?)

84. "She filled their bodies with venom instead of blood,

85. "Grim, monstrous serpents, arrayed in terror,

86. "She decked them with brightness, she fashioned them in exalted forms,

87. "So that fright and horror might overcome him that looked upon them,

88. "So that their bodies might rear up, and no man resist their attack.

89. "She set up the Viper, and the Snake, and the god Lakhamu,

90. "The Whirlwind, the Ravening Dog, the Scorpion-man,

91. "The Storm-wind, the Fish-man, the Horned Beast,

92. "They carried the Weapon which spared not, nor flinched from the battle.

93. "Most mighty were Tiâmat's allies, they could not be resisted.

94. "Thus she caused Eleven [monsters] of this kind to come into being.

95. "Amongst the gods, her first-born son who had collected her company,

96. "That is to say, Kingu, she set on high, she made him the great one among them.

97. "Leader of the hosts in the battle, disposer of the troops,

98. "Bearer of the firmly-grasped weapon, attacker in the fight,

99. "He who in the battle is the master of the weapon

100. "She appointed, she made him to sit down in [goodly apparel],

101. "[Saying]: 'I have recited the incantation for thee, I have magnified thee in the assembly of the gods.

102. "'I have filled his (*i.e.*, thy) hand with the sovereignty of the whole company of the gods.

103. "'Mayest thou be magnified, thou who art my only spouse.

104. "'May the Anunnaki make great thy renown over all of them.'

105. "She gave him the TABLET OF DESTINIES, she fastened it on his head [saying]:

106. "'As for thee, thy command shall not fall empty, what goeth forth from thy mouth shall be established.'

107. "When Kingu was raised on high, and had taken the heavens (Anutum)

108. "He fixed the destinies for the gods, his sons, [saying]:

109. "'Open your mouths, let the Fire-god be quenched,

110. "'He who is glorious in battle and is most mighty shall do great deeds.

111. "'I sent the god Anu, but he could not prevail against her.

112. "'Nudimmud (*i.e.*, Ea) was afraid and turned back.

113. "'Marduk, your son, the envoy of the gods, hath set out.

114. "'His heart is stirred up to oppose Tiâmat.

115. "'He opened his mouth, he spoke unto me, [saying]:

116. "'Should I as your avenger

117. "'Slay Tiâmat, and bestow life upon you,

118. "'Summon a meeting (*i.e.*, council), proclaim and magnify my position,

119. "'Sit down together in friendly fashion in Upshukkinaku,

120. "'Let me issue decrees by the opening of my mouth, even as ye do,

121. "'Whatsoever I bring to pass let it remain unaltered.

122. "'That which my mouth uttereth shall neither fail nor be brought to nought.'"

123. "Hasten ye therefore, issue your decrees speedily

124. "That he may go to meet your mighty enemy."

125. The gods Lakhmu and Lakhamu heard, they wailed loudly,

126. All the Igigi gods wept bitterly [saying]:

127. "Who were [our] enemies until [the gods] were posted [in heaven]?

128. "We cannot comprehend the work of Tiâmat."

129. They gathered themselves together, they went,

130. All the great gods, who issue decrees.

131. They entered in, they filled [the court] before Anshar.

132. Brother [god] kissed brother [god] in the [divine] assembly,

133. They held a meeting, they sat down to a feast,

134. They ate bread, they heated the [sesame wine],

135. The taste of the sweet drink confused their ...

136. They drank themselves drunk, their bodies were filled to overflowing,

137. They were overcome by heaviness [of drink], their livers (*i.e.*, spirits) were exalted,

138. They issued the decree for Marduk as their avenger.

FOURTH TABLET

1. They founded for him a majestic canopy,

2. He (*i.e.*, Marduk) seated himself in the seat of kingship in the presence of his fathers [who said unto him]:

3. "Thou art honourable by reason of thy greatness among the gods.

4. "Thy position is unrivalled, the words thou utterest become Anum (*i.e.*, as fixed as the sky).

5. "Thou art honourable by reason of thy greatness among the gods.

6. "Thy position is unrivalled, the words thou utterest become Anum (*i.e.*, as fixed as the sky).

7. "From this day onward thy command shall not be abrogated.

8. "The power to exalt to heaven and to cast down to the earth both shall be in thy hand,

9. "That which goeth forth from thy mouth shall be established, against thy utterance shall be no appeal.

10. "No one among the gods shall overstep thy boundary,

11. "Worship, which is the object of the sanctuary of the gods,

12. "Whensoever they lack [it] shall be forthcoming in thy sanctuary,

51

13. "O god Marduk, thou art our avenger.

14. "We have given unto thee sovereignty over the whole creation,

15. "Thou shalt sit down, in the council thy word shall be exalted,

16. "Thy weapon shall never fall [from thy hands], it shall break the head of thy foe.

17. "Lord, whosoever putteth his trust in thee, spare thou his life,

18. "And the god who deviseth evil, pour thou out his soul."

19. Then a cloak (literally, one cloak) was set in their midst,

20. They addressed the god Marduk their first-born [saying]:

21. "Thou, Lord, shalt hold the foremost position among the gods.

22. "Decree thou the throwing down[32] and the building up,[33] and it shall come to pass.

23. "Speak but the word, and the cloak shall disappear,

24. "Speak a second time and the cloak shall return uninjured."

25. Marduk spoke the word, the cloak disappeared,

26. He spoke a second time, the cloak reappeared.

27. When the gods his fathers saw the issue of the utterance of his mouth

28. They rejoiced and adored [him, saying], "Marduk is King."

29. They conferred upon him the sceptre, the throne, and the symbol of royalty (?)[34]

30. They gave him the unrivalled weapon, the destroyer of the enemy [saying]:

31. "Go, cut off the life of Tiâmat.

---

[32] *I.e.*, the destruction of Tiâmat.
[33] *I.e.*, the establishing of a new creation to take the place of the old.
[34] The meaning of ⌁ *pal-a* is unknown.

32. "Let the wind carry her blood into the depth [under the earth]."

33. The gods, his fathers, issued the decree for the god Bel.

34. They set him on the road which leadeth to peace and adoration.

35. He strung [his] bow, he set ready his weapon [in the stand],

36. He slung his spear, he attached it to [his belly],

37. He raised the club, he grasped it in his right hand.

38. The bow and the quiver he hung at his side.[35]

39. He set the lightning in front of him.

40. His body was filled with a glancing flame of fire.

41. He made a net wherewith to enclose Tiâmat.

42. He made the four winds to take up their position so that no part of her might escape,

Portion of a tablet inscribed in Babylonian with a text of the Fourth Tablet of the Creation Series. [No. 93,016.]

---

[35] This equipment of the charioteer is shown on the bas-reliefs.

43. The South wind, the North wind, the East wind, the West wind.

44. He held the net close to his side, the gift of his father Anu,

45. He created the "foul" wind, the storm, the parching blast,

46. The wind of "four," the wind of "seven," the typhoon, the wind incomparable

Portion of a tablet inscribed in Assyrian with a text of the Fourth Tablet of the Creation Series. [K. 3437.]

47. He despatched the seven winds which he had made,

48. To make turbid the inward parts of Tiâmat; they followed in his train.

49. The Lord raised up the wind storm, his mighty weapon.

50. He went up into his chariot, the unequalled and terrible tempest.[36]

51. He equipped it, he yoked thereto a team of four horses,

52. Pawing the ground, champing, foaming [eager to] fly,

53. ... [the odour] of their teeth bore foetidness,

54. They were skilled [in biting], they were trained to trample under foot.

[Lines 55-57 too fragmentary to translate; they continue the description of Marduk's equipment.]

58. His brightness streamed forth, his head was crowned [thereby].

59. He took a direct path, he hastened on his journey.

60. He set his face towards the place of Tiâmat, who was ...

61. On his lips ... he restrained

62. ... his hand grasped.

63. At that moment the gods were gazing upon him with fixed intensity,

64. The gods, his fathers, gazed upon him, they gazed upon him.

65. The Lord approached, he looked upon the middle of Tiâmat,

66. He searched out the plan of Kingu, her husband.

67. Marduk looked, Kingu staggered in his gait,

68. His will was destroyed, his motion was paralysed.

69. And the gods his helpers who were marching by his side

70. Saw the [collapse of] their chief and their sight was troubled.

71. Tiâmat [shrieked but] did not turn her head.

72. With lips full of [rebellious words] she maintained her stubbornness

---

36 Compare Psalms xviii, 7-15; civ, i ff.

73. [Saying], "... that thou hast come as the Lord of the gods, [forsooth],

74. "They have appointed thee in the place which should be theirs."

75. The Lord raised up the wind-storm, his mighty weapon,

76. [Against] Tiâmat, who was furious (?), he sent it, [saying]:

77. "[Thou hast made thyself] mighty, thou art puffed upon high,

78. "Thy heart [hath stirred thee up] to invoke battle

79. "... their fathers ...

80. "...

81. "[Thou hast exalted Kingu to be [thy] husband,

82. "[Thou hast made him to usurp] the attributes of Anu

83. "... thou hast planned evil.

84. "[Against] the gods, my fathers, thou hast wrought evil.

85. "Let now thy troops gird themselves up, let them bind on their weapons.

86. "Stand up! Thou and I, let us to the fight!"

87. On hearing these words Tiâmat

88. Became like a mad thing, her senses became distraught,

89. Tiâmat uttered shrill cries again and again.

90. That on which she stood split in twain at the words,

91. She recited an incantation, she pronounced her spell.

92. The gods of battle demanded their weapons.[37]

93. Tiâmat and Marduk, the envoy of the gods, roused themselves,

94. They advanced to fight each other, they drew nigh in battle.

---

[37] I.e., the gods were impatient to begin the fight.

95. The Lord cast his net and made it to enclose her,

96. The evil wind that had its place behind him he let out in her face.

97. Tiâmat opened her mouth to its greatest extent,

98. Marduk made the evil wind to enter [it] whilst her lips were unclosed.

99. The raging winds filled out her belly,

100. Her heart was gripped, she opened wide her mouth [panting].

101. Marduk grasped the spear, he split up her belly,

102. He clave open her bowels, he pierced [her] heart,

103. He brought her to nought, he destroyed her life.

104. He cast down her carcase, he took up his stand upon it,

105. After Marduk had slain Tiâmat the chief,

106. Her host was scattered, her levies became fugitive,

107. And the gods, her allies, who had marched at her side,

108. Quaked with terror, and broke and ran

109. And betook themselves to flight to save their lives.

110. But they found themselves hemmed in, they could not escape,

111. Marduk tied them up, he smashed their weapons.

112. They were cast into the net, and they were caught in the snare,

113. The ... of the world they filled with [their] cries of grief.

114. They received [Marduk's] chastisement, they were confined in restraint,

115. And [on] the Eleven Creatures which Tiâmat had filled with awfulness,

116. The company of the devils that marched at her ...

117. He threw fetters, he ... their sides.

118. They and their resistance he trod under his feet.

119. The god Kingu who had been magnified over them

120. He crushed, he esteemed him [as little worth] as the god Dugga, (as a dead god?).

121. Marduk took from him the TABLET OF DESTINIES, which should never have been his,

122. He sealed it with a seal[38] and fastened it on his breast

123. After he had crushed and overthrown his enemies,

124. He made the haughty enemy to be like the dust underfoot.

125. He established completely Anshar's victory over the enemy,

126. The valiant Marduk achieved the object of Nudimmud (Ea),[39]

127. He imposed strict restraint on the gods whom he had made captive.

128. He turned back to Tiâmat whom he had defeated,

129. The Lord [Marduk] trampled on the rump of Tiâmat,

130. With his unsparing club he clave her skull.

131. He slit open the channels (i.e., arteries) of her blood.

132. He caused the North Wind to carry it away to a place underground.

133. His fathers (i.e., the gods) looked on, they rejoiced, they were glad.

134. They brought unto him offerings of triumph and peace,

135. The Lord [Marduk] paused, he examined Tiâmat's carcase.

---

[38] By impressing his seal on the Tablet Marduk proved his ownership of the Tablet, and made his claim to it legal.
[39] This is an oblique way of saying that Marduk succeeded where Ea failed.

136. He separated flesh [from] hair,[40] he worked cunningly.

137. He slit Tiâmat open like a flat (?) fish [cut into] two pieces,

138. The one half he raised up and shaded the heavens therewith,

139. He pulled the bolt, he posted a guard,

140. He ordered them not to let her water escape.

141. He crossed heaven, he contemplated the regions thereof.

142. He betook himself to the abode of Nudimmud (Ea) that is opposite to the Deep (Apsu),

143. The Lord Marduk measured the dimensions of the Deep,

144. He founded E-Sharra, a place like unto it,

145. The abode E-Sharra, which he made to be heaven.

146. He made the-gods Anu, Bel and Ea to inhabit their [own] cities.

FIFTH TABLET

1. He appointed the Stations for the great gods,

2. He set in heaven the Stars of the Zodiac which are their likenesses.

3. He fixed the year, he appointed the limits thereof.

4. He set up for the twelve months three stars apiece.

5. According to the day of the year he ... figures.

6. He founded the Station of Nibir (Jupiter) to settle their boundaries,

---

[40] The word is kupu, i.e., "reed" or "sedge." It is possible that Marduk skinned Tiâmat.

7. That none might exceed or fall short.

8. He set the Station of Bel and Ea thereby.

9. He opened great gates under shelter on both sides.

10. He made a strong corridor on the left and on the right.

11. He fixed the zenith in the heavenly vault (?)

12. He gave the god Nannar (*i.e.*, the Moon-god) his brightness and committed the night to his care.

Portion of a tablet inscribed in Assyrian with a text of the Fifth Tablet of the Creation Series. [K. 3567.]

13. He set him for the government of the night, to determine the day

14. Monthly, without fail, he set him in a crown (*i.e.*, disk) [saying]:

15. "At the beginning of the month when thou risest over the land,

16. "Make [thy] horns to project to limit six days [of the month]

17. "On the seventh day make thyself like a crown.

18. "On the fourteenth day ...

[Lines 19-26 dealt further with Marduk's instructions to the Moon-god, but are too fragmentary to translate. After line 26 comes a break in the text of 40 lines; lines 66-74 are too fragmentary to translate, but they seem to have described further acts of Creation.]

75. The gods, his (Marduk's) fathers, looked on the net which he had made,

76. They observed how craftily the bow had been constructed,

77. They extolled the work which he had done.

78. [Then] the god Anu lifted up [the bow] in the company of the gods, 79. He kissed the bow [saying]: "That ..."

80. He proclaimed [the names] of the bow to be as follows:—

81. "Verily, the first is 'Long Wood,' the second is ...

82. "Its third name is 'Bow Star in heaven' ..."

83. He fixed a station for it ...

[Of the remaining 57 lines of this tablet only fragments of 17 lines are preserved, and these yield no connected sense.]

SIXTH TABLET

1. On hearing the words of the gods, the heart of Marduk moved him to carry out the works of a craftsman.

2. He opened his mouth, he spake to Ea that which he had planned in his heart, he gave counsel [saying]:

3. "I will solidify blood, I will form bone.

4. "I will set up man, 'Man' [shall be] his name.

5. "I will create the man 'Man.'

6. "The service of the gods shall be established, and I will set them (*i.e.*, the gods) free.

7. "I will make twofold the ways of the gods, and I will beautify [them].

8. "They are [now] grouped together in one place, but they shall be partitioned in two."[41]

9. Ea answered and spake a word unto him

10. For the consolation of the gods[42] he repeated unto him a word of counsel [saying]:

11. "Let one brother [god of their number] be given, let him suffer destruction that men may be fashioned.

12. "Let the great gods be assembled, let this [chosen] one be given in order that they (*i.e.*, the other gods) may be established."

13. Marduk assembled the great gods, [he came near] graciously, he issued a decree,

14. He opened his mouth, he addressed the gods; the King spake a word unto the Anunnaki [saying]:

15. "Verily, that which I spake unto you aforetime was true.

16. "[This time also] I speak truth. [Some there were who] opposed me.[43]

17. "Who was it that created the strife,

18. "Who caused Tiâmat to revolt, to join battle with me?

19. "Let him who created the strife be given [as sacrifice],

20. "I will cause the axe in the act of sinking to do away his sin."

---

[41] Reading, ishtenish lu kuppudu-ma ana shina lu uzizu.
[42] I.e., "to cause the gods to be content,"
[43] Literally "they (indefinite) opposed me."

21. The great gods, the Igigi, answered him,

22. Unto the King of the gods of heaven and of earth, the Prince of the gods, their lord [they said]:

23. "[It was] Kingu who created the strife,

24. "Who made Tiâmat to revolt, to join battle [with thee]."

25. They bound him in fetters [they brought] him before Ea, they inflicted punishment on him, they let his blood,

26. From his blood he (*i.e.*, Ea) fashioned mankind for the service of the gods, and he set the gods free.

27. After Ea had fashioned man he ... laid service upon him.

28. [For] that work, which pleased him not, man was chosen: Marduk ...

29. Marduk, the King of the gods, divided ... he set the Anunnaki up on high.

30. He laid down for Anu a decree that protected [his] heart ... as a guard.

31. He made twofold the ways on the earth [and in the heavens?] 32. By decrees ...

33. The Anunnaki who ...

34. The Anunnaki ...

35. They spake unto Marduk, their lord, [saying]:

36. "O thou Moon-god[44] (Nannaru), who hast established our splendour,

37. "What benefit have we conferred upon thee?

38. "Come, let us make a shrine, whose name shall be renowned;

39. "Come [at] night, our time of festival, let us take our ease therein,

---

[44] See Cuneiform Texts, Part XXIV, Plate 50, where it is said that the god Sin is "Marduk, who maketh bright the night."

40. "Come, the staff shall rule ...

41. "On the day that we reach [thereto] we will take our ease therein."

42. On hearing this Marduk ...

43. The features of his face [shone like] the day exceedingly.

44. [He said),[45] "Like unto ... Babylon, the construction whereof ye desire

45. "I will make ... a city, I will fashion a splendid shrine."

46. The Anunnaki worked the mould [for making bricks], their bricks were ...

47. In the second year [the shrine was as high as] a hill, and the summit of E-Sagila reached the [celestial] Ocean.

48. They made the ziggurat[46] [to reach] the celestial Ocean; unto Marduk, Enlil, Ea [shrines] they appointed,

49. It (*i.e.*, the ziggurat) stood before them majestically: at the bottom and [at the top] they observed its two horns.[47]

50. After the Anunnaki had finished the construction of E-Sagila, and had completed the making of their shrines,

51. They gathered together from the ... of the Ocean (Apsu). In BAR-MAH, the abode which they had made,

52. He (*i.e.*, Marduk) made the gods his fathers to take their seats ... [saying]: "This Babylon shall be your abode.

53. "No mighty one [shall destroy] his house, the great gods shall dwell therein.

---

[45] Lines 44 and 45 announce Marduk's determination to build Babylon.

[46] This is the word commonly used for "temple-tower." The famous ziggurat of E-Sagila here mentioned was built in Seven Stages or Steps, each probably having its own distinctive colour. It was destroyed probably soon after the capture of Babylon by Cyrus (539 B.C.) and when Alexander the Great reached Babylon he found it ruins.

[47] This is the first known mention of the "horns" of a ziggurat, and the exact meaning of the word is doubtful.

[After line 53 the middle portions of several lines of text are obliterated, but from what remains of it is clear that the gods partook of a meal of consecration of the shrine of E-Sagila, and then proceeded to issue decrees. Next Marduk assigns seats to the Seven Gods of Fate and to Enlil and Anu, and then he lays up in E-Sagila the famous bow which he bore during his fight against Tiâmat. When the text again becomes connected we find the gods singing a hymn of praise to Marduk.]

94. "Whatever is ... those gods and goddesses shall bear(?)

95. "They shall never forget, they shall cleave to the god (?)

96. "... they shall make bright, they shall make shrines.

97. "Verily, the decision (concerning) the Black-headed [belongeth to] the gods

98. "... all our names have they called, he (Marduk) is most holy (elli)

99. "... they proclaimed and venerated (?) his names.

100. "His ... is exceedingly bright, his work is ...

101. "Marduk, whose father Anu proclaimed [his name] from his birth,

102. "Who hath set the day at his door ... his going,

103. "By whose help the storm wind was bound ...

104. "Delivered the gods his fathers in the time of trouble.

105. "Verily, the gods have proclaimed his sonship.

106. "In his bright light let them walk for ever.

107. "[On] men whom he hath formed, the created things fashioned by his fingers

108. "He hath imposed the service of the gods, and them he hath set free

109. "...

110. "... they looked at him,

111. "[He is] the far-seeing *(maruķu)* god, verily ...

112. "Who hath made glad the hearts of the Anunnaki, who hath made them to ...

113. "The god Marudukku (⸺ cuneiform ⸺)— verily, he is the object of trust of his country ...

114. "Let men praise him ...

115. "The 'King of the Protecting Heart,' (?) ⸺ cuneiform ⸺, hath arisen and hath [bound] the Serpent ...

116. "Broad is his heart, mighty [his] belly.

117. "King of the gods of heaven and of earth, whose name our company hath proclaimed,

118. "We will fulfil (?) the utterance of his mouth. Over his fathers the gods,

119. "Yea, [over] the gods of heaven and earth, all of them,

120. "His kingship [we will exalt].

121. "[We] will look unto the King of all the heaven and the earth at night when the place of all the gods is darkness (literally sadness).

122. "He hath assigned our dwelling in heaven and in earth in the time of trouble,

123. "He hath allotted stations to the Igigi and the Anunnaki.

124. "The gods themselves are magnified by his name; may he direct their sanctuaries.

125. "ASAR-LU-DUG, ⸺ cuneiform ⸺, is his name by which his father Anu hath named him.

126. "Verily, he is the light of the gods, the mighty ...

127. "Who ... all the parts of heaven and of the land

128. "By a mighty combat he saved our dwelling in the time of trouble.

129. "ASAR-LU-DUG, the god who made him (*i.e.* man) to live, did the god ... call him in the second place

130. "[And] the gods who had been formed, whom he fashioned as though [they were] his offspring.

131. "He is the Lord who hath made all the gods to live by his holy mouth."

[Lines 132-139 are too fragmentary to translate, but it is clear from the text that remains that Lakhmu, and Lakhamu, and Anshar all proclaimed the names of Marduk. When the text again becomes connected Marduk has just been addressing the gods.]

140. In Up-shukkinaku[48] he appointed their council for them.

141. [They said]:—"Of [our] son, the Hero, our Avenger,

142. "We will exalt the name by our speech."

143. They sat down and in their assembly they proclaimed his rank.

144. Every one of them pronounced his name in the sanctuary.

SEVENTH TABLET

1. O ASARI,—giver of plantations, appointer of sowing time,

2. Who dost make grain and fibrous plants, who makest garden herbs to spring up.

3. O ASARU-ALIM—who art weighty in the council-chamber, who art fertile in counsel,

---

[48] From this text it seems clear that Up-shukkinaku was the name of a chamber in the temple of E-Sagila. This name probably means the "chamber of the shakkanaku," i.e., the chamber in which the governor of the city (shakkanaku) went annually to embrace the hands of the god Bel-Marduk, from whom he thereby received the right of sovereignty over the country.

4. To whom the gods pay worship (?) reverent ...

5. O ASARU-ALIM-NUNA—the adored light of the Father who begat him,

6. Who makest straight the direction of Anu, Bel, [and Ea].[49]

7. He is their patron who fixed [their] ...

8. Whose drink is abundance, who goeth forth ...

9. O TUTU—creator of their new life,

10. Supplier of their wants, that they may be satisfied [or, glad],

11. Let but [Tutu] recite an incantation, the gods shall be at rest;

12. Let but [the gods] attack him (*i.e.*, Tutu) in wrath, he shall resist them successfully;

13. Let him be raised up on a high throne in the assembly of the gods....

14. None among the gods is like unto him.

15. O god TUTU, who art the god ZI-UKKINA, life of the host of the gods,

16. Who stablished the shining heavens for the gods,

17. He founded their paths, he fixed [their courses].

18. Never shall his deeds be forgotten among men.

19. O god TUTU, who art ZI-AZAG, was the third name they gave him—holder (*i.e.*, possessor) of holiness,

20. God of the favourable wind, lord of adoration and grace,

21. Creator of fulness and abundance, stablisher of plenty,

22. Who turneth that which is little into that which is much.

---

[49] This line seems to imply that Marduk was regarded as the instructor of the "old" gods; the allusion is, probably, to the "ways" of Anu, Bel and Ea, which are treated as technical terms in astrology.

23. In sore straits we have felt his favouring breeze.

24. Let them (the gods) declare, let them magnify, let them sing his praises.

25. O TUTU, who art the god AGA-AZAG in the fourth place—let men exult.

26. Lord of the holy incantation, who maketh the dead to live,

27. He felt compassion for the gods who were in captivity.

28. He riveted on the gods his enemies the yoke which had been resting on them.

29. In mercy towards them he created mankind,

30. The Merciful One in whose power it is to give life.

31. His words shall endure for ever, they shall never be forgotten,

32. In the mouth of the Black-headed[50] whom his hands have made.

33. O God TUTU, who art the god MU-AZAG in the fifth place—let their mouth recite a holy incantation [to him],

34. Who by his own holy incantation hath destroyed all the evil ones.

35. O god SHAZU, the wise heart of the gods, who searchest the inward parts of the belly,

36. Who dost not permit the worker of evil to go forth by his side,

37. Establisher of the company of the gods ... their hearts.

38. Reducer of the disobedient ...

[Lines 39-106 are wanting. The positions of the fragmentary lines supplied by duplicate fragments are uncertain; in any case they give no connected sense.]

---

[50] Here the title "Black-headed" refers to all mankind, but it is sometimes used by the scribes to distinguish the population of the Euphrates Valley from foreign peoples of light complexions.

Portion of a tablet inscribed in Assyrian with a text of the Seventh Tablet of the Creation Series. [K. 8522.]

107. Verily, he holdeth the beginning and the end of them,[51] verily ...

108. Saying, "He who entered into the middle of Tiâmat resteth not;

109. "His name shall be 'Nibiru' the seizer of the middle.

110. "He shall set the courses of the stars of the heavens,

111. "He shall herd together the whole company of the gods like sheep.

112. "He shall [ever] take Tiâmat captive, he shall slit up her treasure (variant, life), he shall disembowel her."[52]

---

[51] Compare the language of the Kur'ân (Surah II, v. 256), "He (Allah) knoweth what is before them and what is behind them."

113. Among the men who are to come after a lapse of time,

114. Let [these words] be heard without ceasing, may they reign to all eternity,

115. Because he made the [heavenly] places and moulded the stable [earth].

116. Father Bel proclaimed his name, "Lord of the Lands."

117. All the Igigi repeated the title.

118. Ea heard and his liver rejoiced,

119. Saying, "He whose title hath rejoiced his fathers

120. "Shall be even as I am; his name shall be Ea.

121. "He shall dispose of all the magical benefits of my rites,

122. "He shall make to have effect my instructions."

123. By the title of "Fifty times" the great gods

124. Proclaimed his names fifty times, they magnified his going.

EPILOGUE

125. Let the first comer take them and repeat them;

126. Let the wise man and the learned man meditate upon all of them;

127. The father shall repeat them to his son that he may lay hold upon them.

128. Let them (*i.e.*, the names) open the ears of the shepherd and the herdsman.[53]

---

[52] These lines suggest that the fight between Marduk and Tiâmat was recurrent; it is incorrect to translate the verbal forms as preterites.
[53] "To open the ears" — to give understanding.

129. Let [man] rejoice in Marduk, the Lord of the Gods,

130. That his land may be fertile and he himself abide in security.

131. His word is true, his command altereth not.

132. No god hath ever brought to the ground that which issueth from his mouth.

133. They (*i.e.*, the gods) treated him with contempt, he turned not his back [in flight],

134. No god could resist his wrath at its height.

135. His heart is large, his bowels of mercy are great.

136. Of sin and wickedness before him ...

137. The first comer utters his complaint of humiliation before him.

[Lines 138-142 are too fragmentary to translate.]

1. There are in the British Museum several fragments of Neo-Babylonian copies of the Seven Tablets of Creation, the exact position of which is at present uncertain. One of these (S. 2013) is of some importance because it speaks of one object which was in the "upper Tiâmat" ⸗𒀹 𒀸 𒂍 𒇲 ⸗𒀹, and of another which was in the "lower Tiâmat" ⸗𒀹 𒀸 𒄷 𒇲 ⸗𒀹. This shows that the Babylonians thought that one half of the body of Tiâmat, which was split up by Marduk, was made into the celestial ocean, and the other half into the terrestrial ocean, in other words, into "the waters that were above" and "the waters that were beneath" the firmament respectively.

2. When George Smith published his *Chaldean Account of Genesis* in 1876, he was of opinion that the Creation Tablets in the British Museum contained descriptions of the Temptation of Eve by the serpent and of the building and overthrow of the Tower of Babel. The description of Paradise in Genesis ii seems to show traces of Babylonian influence, and the cylinder seal, Brit. Mus. No. 89,326, was thought to be proof that a Babylonian legend of the Temptation existed. In fact, George Smith printed a copy of the seal in his book (p. 91). But it is now known that the tablet which was believed to refer to man's eating of the fruit of the Tree of Knowledge (K. 3, 473 + 79-7-8, 296 + R. 615) describes the banquet of the gods to which they invited Marduk. In like manner the text on K. 3657, which Smith thought referred to the Tower of Babel, is now known to contain no mention of a tower or building of any sort. It was also thought by him that K. 3364 contained a set of instructions which God gave to Adam and Eve after their creation, but it is now known and admitted by all Assyriologists that the text on this tablet contains moral precepts and has nothing to do with the Creation Series. Enquiries are from time to time made at the Museum for tablets which deal with the Temptation of Eve, and the destruction of the Tower of Babel, and the Divine commands to Adam and Eve; it is perhaps not superfluous to say that nothing of the kind exists.

LOST OF THE NAME OF THE STARS OR SIGNS OF THE ZODIAC, WITH A LIST SHOWING THE MONTH THAT WAS ASSOCIATED WITH EACH STAR IN THE PERSIAN PERIOD

BY SIDNEY SMITH, M.A., and C.J. GADD, M.A., Assistants in the Department.

No. 77,821 (85–4–30, 15).

Month.	Determinative of Star.	Name of the Sign of the Zodiac.	Modern Equivalent.
[cuneiform]	[cuneiform]	[cuneiform]	Goat.
[cuneiform]	[cuneiform]	[cuneiform]	Bull.
[cuneiform]	[cuneiform]	[cuneiform]	
		[cuneiform]	Twins.
[cuneiform]	[cuneiform]	[cuneiform]	Crab.
[cuneiform]	[cuneiform]	[cuneiform]	Lion.
[cuneiform]	[cuneiform]	[cuneiform]	Virgin.
[cuneiform]	[cuneiform]	[cuneiform]	Scales.
[cuneiform]	[cuneiform]	[cuneiform]	Scorpion.
[cuneiform]	[cuneiform]	[cuneiform]	Bow.
[cuneiform]	[cuneiform]	[cuneiform]	Capricornus.
[cuneiform]	[cuneiform]	[cuneiform]	Water-bearer
[cuneiform]	[cuneiform]	[cuneiform]	The Fishes.

TRANSLITERATION.   TRANSLATION.

1	Nisannu	(kakkab) (amel) Agru....	The Labourer.
2	Airu	" Kakkab u (kakkab) Alap shame	The Star and the Bull of heaven.
3	Simanu	" Re'u kinu shame u (kakkab) tu'ame rabuti	The faithful shepherd of heaven and the Great

74

4	Duuzu	" AL.LUL. (shittu)[54]...	The Tortoise.
5	Abu	" Kalbu rabu	Great Dog (Lion).
6	Ululu	" Shiru	Virgin with ear of corn.
7	Tashritum	" Zibanitum	....
8	Araḫ shamna	" Akrabu	The Scorpion.
9	Kislimu	" PA.BIL.SAG	Enurta (the god).
10	Ṭebetum	" SUḪUR.MASH	The Goat-fish.
11	Shabaṭu	" Gula	The Great Star
12	Addaru	" DIL.GAN.u rikis nuni	The star ... and the Band of Fishes.

I have been assisted in the preparation of this monograph by Mr. Sidney Smith, M.A., Assistant in the Department.

E.A. WALLIS BUDGE

DEPARTMENT OF EGYPTIAN AND ASSYRIAN ANTIQUITIES, BRITISH MUSEUM. *June* 1, 1921

---

[54] The Egyptian Sheta

THE BABYLONIAN STORY OF THE DELUGE AS TOLD BY ASSYRIAN TABLETS FROM NINEVEH

THE DISCOVERY OF THE TABLETS AT NINEVEH BY LAYARD, RASSAM AND SMITH

In 1845–47 and again in 1849–51 Mr. (later Sir) A. H. Layard carried out a series of excavations among the ruins of the ancient city of Nineveh, "that great city, wherein are more than sixteen thousand persons that cannot discern between their right hand and their left; and *also* much cattle" (Jonah iv, II). Its ruins lie on the left or east bank of the Tigris, exactly opposite the town of Al-Mawsil, or Môsul, which was founded by the Sassanians and marks the site of Western Nineveh. At first Layard thought that these ruins were not those of Nineveh, which he placed at Nimrûd, about 20 miles downstream, but of one of the other cities that were builded by Asshur (*see* Gen. x, 11, 12). Thanks, however, to Christian, Roman and Muhammadan tradition, there is no room for doubt about it, and the site of Nineveh has always been known. The fortress which the Arabs built there in the seventh century was known as "Kal'at-Nînawî, *i.e.*, "Nineveh Castle," for many centuries, and all the Arab geographers agree in saying that tile mounds opposite Môsul contain the ruins of the palaces and walls of Nineveh. And few of them fail to mention that close by them is "Tall Nabi Yûnis," *i.e.*, the Hill from which the Prophet Jonah preached repentance to the inhabitants of Nineveh, that "exceeding great city of three days' journey" (Jonah iii, 3). Local tradition also declares that the prophet was buried in the Hill, and his supposed tomb is shown there to this day.

76

THE WALLS AND PALACES OF NINEVEH

The situation of the ruins of the palaces of Nineveh is well shown by the accompanying reproduction of the plan of the city made by Commander Felix Jones, I.N. The remains of the older palaces built by Sargon II (B.C. 721–705), Sennacherib (B.C. 705–681), and Esarhaddon (B.C. 681–668) lie under the hill called Nabi Yûnis, and those of the palaces and other buildings of Ashur-bani-pal (B.C. 681–626) under the mound which is known locally as "Tall al-'Armûshîyah," *i.e.*, "The Hill of 'Armûsh," and "Kuyûnjik." The latter name is said to be derived from two Turkish words meaning "many sheep," in allusion to the large flocks of sheep that find their pasture on and about the mound in the early spring. These two great mounds lie close to the remains of the great west wall of Nineveh, which in the time of the last Assyrian Empire was washed by the waters of the river Tigris. At some unknown period the course of the river changed, and it is now more than a mile distant from the city wall. The river Khausur, or Khoser, divides the area of Nineveh into two parts, and passing close to the southern end of Kuyûnjik empties itself into the Tigris. The ruins of the wails of Nineveh show that the east wall was 16,000 feet long, the north wall 7,000 feet long, the west wall 13,600 feet, and the south wall 3,000 feet; its circuit was about 13,200 yards or 7½ miles.

DISCOVERY OF THE LIBRARY OF THE TEMPLE OF NEBO AT NINEVEH

In the spring of 1852 Layard, assisted by H. Rassam, continued the excavation of the "South West Palace" at Kuyûnjik. In one part of the building he found two small chambers, opening into each other, which he called the "chamber of records," or "the house of the rolls." He gave them this name because "to the height of a foot or more from the floor they were entirely filled" with inscribed baked clay tablets and fragments of tablets. Some tablets were complete, but by far the larger number of them had been broken up into many fragments, probably by the falling in of the roof and upper parts of the walls of the buildings when the city was pillaged and set on fire

77

by the Medes and Babylonians. The tablets that were kept in these chambers numbered many thousands. Besides those that were found in them by Layard, large numbers have been dug out all along the corridor which passed the chambers and led to the river, and a considerable number were kicked on to the river front by the feet of the terrified fugitives from the palace when it was set on fire. The tablets found by Layard were of different sizes; the largest were rectangular, flat on one side and convex on the other, and measured about 9 ins. by 6½ ins., and the smallest were about an inch square. The importance of this "find" was not sufficiently recognized at the time, for the tablets, which were thought to be decorated pottery, were thrown into baskets and sent down the river loose on rafts to Basrah, whence they were despatched to England on a British man o' war. During their transport from Nineveh to England they suffered more damage from want of packing than they had suffered from the wrath of the Medes. Among the complete tablets that were found in the two chambers several had colophons inscribed or scratched upon them, and when these were deciphered by Rawlinson, Hincks and Oppert a few years later, it became evident that they had formed part of the library of the *Temple of Nebo at Nineveh.*

NEBO AND HIS LIBRARY AT NINEVEH

Nothing is known of the early history of the Library[55] of the Temple of Nebo at Nineveh. There is little doubt that it was in existence in the reign of Sargon II, and it was probably founded at the instance of the priests of Nebo who were settled at Nimrûd (the Calah of Gen. X, 11), about 20 miles downstream of Nineveh. Authorities differ in their estimate of the attributes that were assigned to Nebo (⊢⊣⊢ ⊢⊡ *Nabu*) in Pre-Babylonian times, and cannot decide whether he was a water-god, or a fire-god, or a corn-god, but he was undoubtedly associated with Marduk, either as his son or as a fellow-god. It is certain that as early as B.C. 2000 he was regarded as one of the "Great Gods" of Babylonia, and about 1,200 years later his cult was general in Assyria. He had a temple at Nimrûd in the ninth century

---

[55] A group of Sumerian words for "library" are ⊲⊬⊦ ⊸⊏⊲ ⌐ (*girginakku*), and these seem to mean "collection of writings."

B.C., and King Adad-Nirari (B.C. 811–783) set up six statues in it to the honour of the god; two of these statues are now in the British Museum. Under the last Assyrian Empire he was believed to possess the wisdom of all the gods, and to be the "All-wise" and "All-knowing." He was the inventor of all the arts and sciences, and the source of inspiration in wise and learned men, and he was the divine scribe and past master of all the mysteries connected with literature and the art of writing (⟨cuneiform⟩, *duppu sharrute*). Ashur-bani-pal addresses him as "Nebo, the beneficent son, the director of the hosts of heaven and of earth, holder of the tablet of knowledge, bearer of the writing-reed of destiny, lengthener of days, vivifier of the dead, stablisher of light for the men who are troubled" (*see* tablet R.M. 132) In the reign of Sargon II the temple library of Nebo was probably housed in some building at or near Nabi Yûnis, or, as George Smith thought, near Kuyûnjik, or at Kuyûnjik itself. As Layard found the remains of Nebo's Library in the South West Palace, it is probable that Ashur-bani-pal built a new temple to Nebo there and had the library transferred to it. Nebo's temple at Nineveh bore the same name as his very ancient temple at Borsippa (the modern Birs-i-Nimrûd), viz., "*E-Zida.*"

DISCOVERY OF THE PALACE LIBRARY OF

ASHUR-BANI-PAL

In the spring of 1852 Layard was obliged to close his excavations for want of funds, and he returned to England with Rassam, leaving all the northern half of the great mound of Kuyûnjik unexcavated. He resigned his position as Director of Excavations to the Trustees of the British Museum, and Colonel (later Sir) H. C. Rawlinson, Consul-General of Baghdâd, undertook to direct any further excavations that might be possible to carry out later on. During the summer the Trustees received a further grant from Parliament for excavations in Assyria, and they dispatched Rassam to finish the exploration of Kuyûnjik, knowing that the lease of the mound of Kuyûnjik for excavation purposes which he had obtained from its owner had several years to run. When Rassam arrived at Môsul in 1853, and was collecting his men for work, he discovered that Rawlinson, who knew nothing about the lease of the mound which

Rassam held, had given the French Consul, M. Place, permission to excavate the northern half of the mound, *i.e.*, that part of it which he was most anxious to excavate for the British Museum. He protested, but in vain, and, finding that M. Place intended to hold Rawlinson to his word, devoted himself to clearing out part of the South West Palace which Layard had attacked in 1852. Meanwhile M. Place was busily occupied with the French excavations at Khorsabad, a mound which contained the ruins of the great palace of Sargon II, and had no time to open up excavations at Kuyûnjik. In this way a year passed, and as M. Place made no sign that he was going to excavate at Kuyûnjik and Rassam's time for returning to England was drawing near, the owner of the mound, who was anxious to get the excavations finished so that he might again graze his flocks on the mound, urged Rassam to get to work in spite of Rawlinson's agreement with M. Place. He and Rassam made arrangements to excavate the northern part of the mound clandestinely and by night, and on 20th December, 1853, the work began. On the first night nothing of importance was found; on the second night the men uncovered a portion of a large bas-relief; and on the third night a huge mass of earth collapsed revealing a very fine bas-relief, sculptured with a scene representing Ashur-bani-pal standing in his chariot. The news of the discovery was quickly carried to all parts of the neighbourhood, and as it was impossible to keep the diggings secret any longer, the work was continued openly and by day. The last-mentioned bas-relief was one of the series that lined the chamber, which was 50 feet long and 15 feet wide, and illustrated a royal lion hunt.[56] This series, that is to say, all of it that the fire which destroyed the palace had spared, is now in the British Museum (*see* the Gallery of the Assyrian Saloon).

Whilst the workmen were clearing out the Chamber of the Lion Hunt they came across several heaps of inscribed baked clay tablets of "all shapes and sizes," which resembled in general appearance the tablets that Layard had found in the South West Palace the year before. There were no remains with them, or near them, that suggested they had been arranged systematically and stored in the Chamber of the Lion Hunt, and it seems as if they had been brought

---

[56] These bas-reliefs show that lions were kept in cages in Nineveh and let out to be killed by the King with his own hand. There seems to be an allusion to the caged lions by Nahum (ii. 11) who says, "Where is the dwelling of the lions, and the feeding place of the young lions, where the lion, *even* the old lion, walked, *and* the lion's whelp, and none made *them* afraid?"

80

there from another place and thrown down hastily, for nearly all of them were broken into small pieces. As some of them bore traces of having been exposed to great heat they must have been in that chamber during the burning of the palace. When the tablets were brought to England and were examined by Rawlinson, it was found from the information supplied by the colophons that they formed a part of the great *Private Library of Ashur-bani-pal*, which that king kept in his palace. The tablets found by Layard in 1852 and by Rassam in 1853 form the unique and magnificent collection of cuneiform tablets in the British Museum, which is now commonly known as the "Kuyûnjik Collection." The approximate number of the inscribed baked clay tablets and fragments that have come from Kuyûnjik and are now in the British Museum is 25,073. It is impossible to over-estimate their importance and value from religious, historical and literary points of view; besides this, they have supplied the material for the decipherment of cuneiform inscriptions in the Assyrian, Babylonian and Sumerian languages, and form the foundation of the science of Assyriology which has been built up with such conspicuous success during the last 70 years.

ASHUR-BANI-PAL, BOOK-COLLECTOR AND PATRON OF LEARNING

Ashur-bani-pal (the Asnapper of Ezra iv, 10) succeeded his father Esarhaddon B.C. 668, and at a comparatively early period of his reign he seems to have devoted himself to the study of the history of his country, and to the making of a great Private Library. The tablets that have come down to us prove not only that he was as great a benefactor of the Library of the Temple of Nebo as any of his predecessors, but that he was himself an educated man, a lover of learning, and a patron of the literary folk of his day. In the introduction to his Annals as found inscribed on his great ten-sided cylinder in the British Museum he tells us how he took up his abode in the chambers of the palace from which Sennacherib and Esarhaddon had ruled the Assyrian Empire, and in describing his own education he says:

81

"I, Ashur-bani-pal, within it (*i.e.*, the palace) understood the wisdom of Nebo, all the art of writing of every craftsman, of every kind, I made myself master of them all (*i.e.*, of the various kinds of writing)."[57]

These words suggest that Ashur-bani-pal could not only read cuneiform texts, but could write like a skilled scribe, and that he also understood all the details connected with the craft of making and baking tablets. Having determined to form a Library in his palace he set to work in a systematic manner to collect literary works. He sent scribes to ancient seats of learning, *e.g.*, Ashur, Babylon, Cuthah, Nippur, Akkad, Erech, to make copies of the ancient works that were preserved there, and when the copies came to Nineveh he either made transcripts of them himself, or caused his scribes to do so for the Palace Library. In any case he collated the texts himself and revised them before placing them in his Library. The appearance of the tablets from his Library suggests that he established a factory in which the clay was cleaned and kneaded and made into homogeneous, well-shaped tablets, and a kiln in which they were baked, after they had been inscribed. The uniformity of the script upon them is very remarkable, and texts with mistakes in them are rarely found. How the tablets were arranged in the Library is not known, but certainly groups were catalogued, and some tablets were labelled.[58] Groups of tablets were arranged in numbered series, with "catch lines," the first tablet of the series giving the first line of the second tablet, the second tablet giving the first line of the third tablet, and so on.

Ashur-bani-pal was greatly interested in the literature of the Sumerians, *i.e.*, the non-Semitic people who occupied Lower Babylonia about B.C. 3500 and later. He and his scribes made bilingual lists of signs and words and objects of all classes and kinds, all of which are of priceless value to the modern student of the Sumerian and Assyrian languages. Annexed is an extract from a List of Signs with Sumerian and Assyrian values. The signs of which

---

[57] [cuneiform signs]

[cuneiform signs]

[cuneiform signs] (Brit. Mus., No. 91,026, Col. 1, ll. 31–33).

[58] K. 1352 is a good specimen of a catalogue (see p. 10); K. 1400 and K. 1539 are labels (see p. 12).

the meanings are given are in the middle column; the Sumerian values are given in the column to the left, and their meanings in Assyrian in the column to the right. To many of his copies of Sumerian hymns, incantations, magical formulas, etc., Ashur-bani-pal caused interlinear translations to be added in Assyrian, and of such bilingual documents the following extract from a text relating to the Seven Evil Spirits will serve as a specimen. The 1st, 3rd, 5th, etc., lines are written in Sumerian, and the 2nd, 4th, 6th, etc., lines in Assyrian.

Extract from a List of Signs with Sumerian and Assyrian values. From Rawlinson, Cuneiform Inscriptions of Western Asia, Vol. II, Plate I, ll. 155–168.

Extract from a tablet containing a text relating to the Seven Evil Spirits, written in the Sumerian language, with an interlinear translation in Assyrian. From Rawlinson, Cuneiform Inscription of Western Asia, Vol. IV, Plate XV, Obverse, ll. 33–46 (K. III–K. 2754).

The tablets that belonged to Ashur-bani-pal's private Library and those of the Temple of Nebo can be distinguished by the colophons, when these exist. Two forms of colophon for each class of the two great collections of tablets are known, one short and one long. The short colophon on the tablets of the King's Library reads:—"Palace of Ashur-bani-pal, king of hosts, king of the country of Assyria" , and that on the tablets of the Library of Nebo reads:—"[Country of ?] Ashur-bani-pal, king of hosts, king of the country of Assyria" . See on the Tablet of Astrological Omens, p. 136. The longer colophons are of considerable interest and renderings of two typical examples are here appended:—

Colophon of a tablet from the Palace Library of Ashur-bani-pal
containing incantations in the Sumerian language, with interlinear
translations in Assyrian. For an English rendering see following
page. From Rawlinson, *Cuneiform Inscriptions of Western Asia*,
Vol. IV, Plate VI, col. 6 (K. 4870).

1

COLOPHON OF THE TABLETS OF THE PALACE LIBRARY (K. 4870.)

1. Palace of Ashur-bani-pal, king of hosts, king of the country of Assyria,

2. who trusteth in the god Ashur and the goddess Bêlit,

3. on whom the god Nebo (Nabû) and the goddess Tasmetu

4. have bestowed all-hearing ears

5. and his possession of eyes that are clearsighted,

6. and the finest results of the art of writing

7. which, among the kings who have gone before,

8. no one ever acquired that craft.

9. The wisdom of Nebo [as expressed in] writing, of every kind,

10. on tablets I wrote, collated and revised,

11. [and] for examination and reading

12. in my palace I placed—[I]

13. the prince who knoweth the light of the king of the gods, Ashur.

14. Whosoever shall carry [them] off, or his name side by side with mine

15. shall write may Ashur and Bêlit wrathfully

16. sweep away, and his name and his seed destroy in the land.

COLOPHON OF THE TABLETS OF
THE LIBRARY OF NEBO (RM. 132.)

1. To Nebo, beneficent son, director of the hosts of heaven and of earth,

2. holder of the tablet of knowledge, he who hath grasped the writing reed of destinies,

3. lengthener of days, vivifier of the dead, stablisher of light for the men who are perplexed,

4. [from] the great lord, the noble Ashur-bani-pal, the lord, the approved of the gods Ashur, Bêl and Nebo,

5. the shepherd, the maintainer of the holy places of the great gods, stablisher of their revenues,

6. son of Esarhaddon, king of hosts, king of Assyria,

7. grandson of Sennacherib, king of hosts, king of Assyria,

8. for the life of his souls, length of his days, [and] well-being of his posterity,

9. to make permanent the foundation of his royal throne, to hear his supplications,

10. to receive his petitions, to deliver into his hands the rebellious.

11. The wisdom of Ea, the precious priesthood, the leadership,

12. what is composed for the contentment of the heart of the great gods,

13. I wrote upon tablets, I collated, I revised

14. literally according to all the tablets of the lands of Ashur and Akkad,

15. and I placed in the Library of E-Zida, the temple of Nebo my lord, which is in Nineveh.

16. O Nebo, lord of the hosts of heaven and of earth, look upon that Library joyfully for years (*i.e.*, for ever).

17. Of Ashur-bani-pal, the chief, the worshipper of thy divinity, daily the reward of the offering—

18. his life decree, so that he may exalt thy great godhead.

The tablets from both Libraries when unbroken vary in size from 15 inches by 8⅝ inches to 1 inch by ⅞ inch, and they are usually about 1 inch thick. In shape they are rectangular, the obverse being flat and tile reverse slightly convex. Contract tablets, letter tablets and "case" tablets are very much smaller, and resemble small pillows in shape. The principal subjects dealt with in the tablets are history, annalistic or summaries, letters, despatches, reports, oracles, prayers, contracts, deeds of sale of land, produce, cattle, slaves, agreements, dowries, bonds for interest (with impressions of seals, and fingernails, or nail marks), chronography, chronology, Canons of Eponyms, astrology (forecasts, omens, divinations, charms, spells, incantations), mythology, legends, grammar, law, geography, etc.[59]

GEORGE SMITH'S DISCOVERY OF THE EPIC OF GILGAMISH AND THE STORY OF THE DELUGE

The mass of tablets which had been discovered by Layard and Rassam at Nineveh came to the British Museum in 1854–5, and their examination by Rawlinson and Norris began very soon after. Mr. Bowler, a skilful draughtsman and copyist of tablets, whom

---

[59] For a full description of the general contents of the two great Libraries of Nineveh, see Bezold, Catalogue of the Cuneiform Tablets of the Kouyûnjik. Collection, Vol. V., London, 1899, p. xviiiff.; and King, Supplement, London, 1914, p. xviiiff.

Rawlinson employed in making transfers of copies of cuneiform texts for publication by lithography, rejoined a considerable number of fragments of bilingual lists, syllabaries, etc., which were published in the second volume of the *Cuneiform Inscriptions of Western Asia*, in 1866. In that year the Trustees of the British Museum employed George Smith to assist Rawlinson in sorting, classifying and rejoining fragments, and a comprehensive examination of the collection by him began. His personal interest in Assyriology was centred upon historical texts, especially those which threw any light on the Bible Narrative. But in the course of his search for stories of the campaigns of Sargon II, Sennacherib, Esarhaddon and Ashur-bani-pal, he discovered among other important documents (1) a series of portions of tablets which give the adventures of Gilgamish, an ancient king of Erech; (2) An account of the Deluge, which is supplied by the Eleventh Tablet of the Legend of Gilgamish (in more than one version); (3) A detailed description of the Creation; (4) the Legend of the Descent of Ishtar into Hades in quest of Tammuz. The general meaning of the texts was quite clear, but there were many gaps in them, and it was not until December, 1872, that George Smith published his description of the Legend of Gilgamish, and a translation of the "Chaldean Account of the Deluge." The interest which his paper evoked was universal, and the proprietors of the "Daily Telegraph" advocated that Smith should be at once dispatched to Nineveh to search for the missing fragments of tablets which would fill up the gaps in his texts, and generously offered to contribute 1,000 guineas towards the cost of the excavations. The Trustees accepted the offer and gave six months' leave of absence to Smith, who left London in January, and arrived in Môsul in March, 1873. In the following May he recovered from Kuyûnjik a fragment that contained "the greater portion of seventeen lines of inscription belonging to the first column of the Chaldean account of the Deluge, and fitting into the only place where there was a serious blank in the story."[60] During the excavations which Smith carried out at Kuyûnjik in 1873 and 1874 he recovered many fragments of tablets, the texts of which enabled him to complete his description of the contents of the Twelve Tablets of the Legend of Gilgamish which included his translation of the story of the Deluge. Unfortunately Smith died of hunger and sickness near Aleppo in 1876, and he was unable to revise his early work, and to supplement it with the information which he had acquired during his latest travels in Assyria and Babylonia. Thanks to the excavations which were carried on at

---

[60] Smith, *Assyrian Discoveries*, London, 1875, p. 97.

Kuyûnjik by the Trustees of the British Museum after his untimely death, several hundreds of tablets and fragments have been recovered, and many of these have been rejoined to the tablets of the older collection. By the careful study and investigation of the old and new material Assyriologists have, during the last forty years, been enabled to restore and complete many passages in the Legends of Gilgamish and the Flood. It is now clear that the Legend of the Flood had not originally any connection with the Legend of Gilgamish, and that it was introduced into it by a late editor or redactor of the Legend, probably in order to complete the number of the Twelve Tablets on which it was written in the time of Ashur-bani-pal.

THE LEGEND OF THE DELUGE IN
BABYLONIA

In the introduction to his paper on the "Chaldean Account of the Deluge," which Smith read in December, 1872, and published in 1873, he stated that the Assyrian text which he had found on Ashur-bani-pal's tablets was copied from an archetype at Erech in Lower Babylonia. This archetype was, he thought, "either written in, or translated into Semitic Babylonian, at a very early period," and although he could not assign a date to it, he adduced a number of convincing proofs in support of his opinion. The language in which he assumed the Legend to have been originally composed was known to him under the name of "Accadian," or "Akkadian," but is now called "Sumerian." Recent research has shown that his view on this point was correct on the whole. But there is satisfactory proof available to show that versions or recensions of the Legend of the Deluge and of the Epic of Gilgamish existed both in Sumerian and Babylonian, as early as B.C. 2000. The discovery has been made of a fragment of a tablet with a small portion of the Babylonian version of the Legend of the Deluge inscribed upon it, and dated in a year which is the equivalent of the 11th year of Ammisaduga, *i.e.* about B.C. 2000.[61] And in the Museum at Philadelphia[62] is preserved half

---

[61] Published by Scheil in Maspero's Recueil, Vol. XX, p. 55ff.

of a tablet which when whole contained a complete copy of the Sumerian version of the Legend, and must have been written about the same date. The fragment of the tablet written in the reign of Ammisaduga is of special importance because the colophon shows that the tablet to which it belonged was the second of a series, and that this series was not that of the Epic of Gilgamish, and from this we learn that in B.C. 2000 the Legend of the Deluge did not form the XIth Tablet of the Epic of Gilgamish, as it did in the reign of Ashur-bani-pal, or earlier. The Sumerian version is equally important, though from another point of view, for the contents and position of the portion of it that remains on the half of the tablet mentioned above make it certain that already at this early period there were several versions of the Legend of the Deluge current in the Sumerian language. The fact is that the Legend of the Deluge was then already so old in Mesopotamia that the scribes added to or abbreviated the text at will, and treated the incidents recorded in it according to local or popular taste, tradition and prejudice. There seems to be no evidence that proves conclusively that the Sumerian version is older than the Semitic, or that the latter was translated direct from the former version. It is probable that both the Sumerians and the Semites, each in their own way, attempted to commemorate an appalling disaster of unparalleled magnitude, the knowledge of which, through tradition, was common to both peoples. It is, at all events, clear that the Sumerians regarded the Deluge as an historic event, which they were, practically, able to date, for some of their tablets contain lists of kings who reigned before the Deluge, though it must be confessed that the lengths assigned to their reigns are incredible.

It is not too much to assume that the original event commemorated in the Legend of the Deluge was a serious and prolonged inundation or flood in Lower Babylonia, which was accompanied by great loss of life and destruction of property. The Babylonian versions state that this inundation or flood was caused by rain, but passages in some of them suggest that the effects of the rainstorm were intensified by other physical happenings connected with the earth, of a most destructive character. The Hebrews also, as we may see from the Bible, had alternative views as to the cause of the Deluge. According to one, rain fell upon the earth for forty days and forty

---

[62] The text is published by A. Poebel with transcription, commentary, etc., in Historical Texts, Philadelphia, 1914, and Historical and Grammatical Texts, Philadelphia, 1914.

nights (Gen. vii, 12), and according to the other the Deluge came because "all the fountains of the "great deep" were broken up, and "the flood-gates of heaven were opened" (Gen. vii, 11). The latter view suggests that the rain flood was joined by the waters of the sea. Later tradition, based partly on Babylonian and partly on Hebrew sources, asserts in the "Cave of Treasures"[63] that when Noah had entered the Ark and the door was shut, "the sluices of heaven were opened, and the deeps were rent asunder," and "that the Ocean, that great sea that surroundeth the whole world, vomited its waters, and the sluices of heaven being opened, and the deeps of the earth being rent asunder, the storehouses of the winds were opened, and the whirlwinds broke loose, and the Ocean roared and poured out its waters in floods." The ark was steered over the waters by an angel who acted as pilot, and when that had come to rest on the mountains of Kardô (Armenia) "God commanded the waters and they separated from each other. The waters that had been above ascended to their place above the heavens, whence they had come; and the waters that had come up from under the earth returned to the lower deep; and the waters that were from the Ocean returned into it" (Brit. Mus. MS. Orient. No. 25,875, fol. 17b, col. 1 and fol. 18a, cols. 1 and 2). Many authorities seeking to find a foundation of fact for the Legend of the Deluge in Mesopotamia have assumed that the rain flood was accompanied either by an earthquake or a tidal wave, or by both. There is no doubt that the cities of Lower Babylonia were nearer the sea in the Sumerian Period than they are at the present time, and it is a generally accepted view that the head of the Persian Gulf lay further to the north at that time. A cyclone coupled with a tidal wave is a sufficient base for any of the forms of the Legend now known.

A comparison of the contents of the various Sumerian and Babylonian versions of the Deluge that have come down to us shows us that they are incomplete. And as none of them tells so connected and full a narrative of the prehistoric shipbuilder as Berosus, a priest of Bêl, the great god of Babylon, it seems that the Mesopotamian scribes were content to copy the Legend in an abbreviated form. Berosus, it is true, is not a very ancient authority, for he was not born until the reign of Alexander the Great, but he was a learned man and was well acquainted with the Babylonian language, and with the ancient literature of his country, and he wrote a history of Babylonia, some fragments of which have been

---

[63] A famous work composed by members of the College of Edessa in the fifth or sixth century A.D.

preserved to us in the works of Alexander Polyhistor, Eusebius, and others. The following is a version of the fragment which describes the flood that took place in the days of Xisuthrus, the tenth King of the Chaldeans, and is of importance for comparison with the rendering of the Legend of the Deluge, as found on the Ninevite tablets, which follows immediately after.

THE LEGEND OF THE DELUGE ACCORDING
TO BEROSUS

"After the death of Ardates, his son Xisuthrus reigned eighteen *sari*. In his time happened a great Deluge; the history of which is thus described. The Deity, Cronus, appeared to him in a vision, and warned him that upon the 15th day of the month Daesius there would be a flood, by which mankind would be destroyed. He therefore enjoined him to write a history of the beginning, procedure and conclusion of all things; and to bury it in the city of the Sun at Sippara; and to build a vessel, and take with him into it his friends and relations; and to convey on board everything necessary to sustain life, together with all the different animals, both birds and quadrupeds, and trust himself fearlessly to the deep. Having asked the Deity, whither he was to sail? he was answered, 'To the Gods': upon which he offered up a prayer for the good of mankind. He then obeyed the divine admonition; and built a vessel 5 stadia in length, and 2 in breadth. Into this he put everything which he had prepared; and last of all conveyed into it his wife, his children, and his friends. After the flood had been upon the earth, and was in time abated, Xisuthrus sent out birds from the vessel; which, not finding any food nor any place whereupon they might rest their feet, returned to him again. After an interval of some days, he sent them forth a second time; and they now returned with their feet tinged with mud. He made a trial a third time with these birds; but they returned to him no more: from whence he judged that the surface of the earth had appeared above the waters. He therefore made an opening in the vessel, and upon looking out found that it was stranded upon the side of some mountain; upon which he immediately quitted it with his wife, his daughter, and the pilot. Xisuthrus then paid his adoration to the earth, and, having constructed an altar, offered sacrifices to the gods, and, with those who had come out of the vessel with him, disappeared. They, who remained within, finding that their companions did not return, quitted the vessel with many lamentations, and called continually on the name of Xisuthrus. Him they saw no more; but they could distinguish his voice in the air, and could hear him admonish them to pay due regard to religion; and likewise informed them that it was upon account of his piety that he was translated to live with the gods; that his wife and daughter, and the pilot, had obtained the same honour. To this he added that they should return to Babylonia; and, it was ordained, search for the writings at Sippara, which they were to make known to mankind: moreover that the place, wherein they then were, was the land of Armenia. The rest having heard these words, offered sacrifices to the gods; and taking a circuit journeyed towards Babylonia." (Cory, *Ancient Fragments*, London, 1832, p. 26ff.)

THE BABYLONIAN LEGEND OF THE DELUGE AS TOLD TO THE HERO GILGAMISH BY HIS ANCESTOR UTA-NAPISHTIM, WHO HAD BEEN MADE IMMORTAL BY THE GODS

The form of the Legend of the Deluge given below is that which is found on the Eleventh of the Series of Twelve Tablets in the Library of Nebo at Nineveh, which described the life and exploits of Gilgamish (⌐╼ ╒╎ ╨╨╫ ╌), an early king of the city of Erech. As we have seen above, the Legend of the Deluge has in reality no connection with the Epic of Gilgamish, but was introduced into it by the editors of the Epic at a comparatively late period, perhaps even during the reign of Ashur-bani-pal (B.C. 668–626). A summary of the contents of the other Tablets of the Gilgamish Series is given in the following section of this short monograph. It is therefore only necessary to state here that Gilgamish, who was horrified and almost beside himself when his bosom friend and companion Enkidu (╾╬ ╫▧ ╤), Eabâni) died, meditated deeply how he could escape death himself. He knew that his ancestor Uta-

Napishtim (⌐ ⌐⌐ ⌐⌐⌐⌐ ⌐⌐⌐) had become immortal, therefore he determined to set out for the place where Uta-Napishtim lived so that he might obtain from him the secret of immortality. Guided by a dream in which he saw the direction of the place where Uta-Napishtim lived, Gilgamish set out for the Mountain of the Sunset, and, after great toil and many difficulties, came to the shore of a vast sea. Here he met Ur-Shanabi (⌐ ⌐⌐⌐ ⌐⌐⌐), the boatman of Uta-Napishtim, who was persuaded to carry him in his boat over the "waters of death" (⌐⌐ ⌐⌐⌐⌐⌐ ⌐⌐ ⌐⌐⌐⌐ ⌐⌐⌐), and at length he landed on the shore of the country of Uta-Napishtim. The immortal came down to the shore and asked the newcomer the object of his visit, and Gilgamish told him of the death of his great friend Enkidu, and of his desire to escape from death and to find immortality. Uta-Napishtim having made to Gilgamish some remarks which seem to indicate that in his opinion death was inevitable,

1. Gilgamish[64] said unto Uta-Napishtim, to Uta-Napishtim the remote:

2. "I am looking at thee, Uta-Napishtim.

3. Thy person is not altered; even as am I so art thou.

4. Verily, nothing about thee is changed; even as am I so art thou.

5. [Moved is my] heart to do battle,

6. But thou art at leisure and dost lie upon thy back.

7. How then wast thou able to enter the company of the gods and see life?"

Thereupon Uta-Napishtim related to Gilgamish the Story of the Deluge, and the Eleventh Tablet continues thus:—

8. Uta-Napishtim said unto him, to Gilgamish:

9. "I will reveal unto thee, O Gilgamish, a hidden mystery,

---

[64] A transcript of the cuneiform text by George Smith, who was the first to translate it, will be found in Rawlinson, Cuneiform Inscriptions of Western Asia, Vol. IV., plates 43 and 44; and a transcript, with transliteration and translation by the late Prof. L. W. King, is given in his First Steps in Assyrian, London, 1898, p. 161ff.

10. And a secret matter of the gods I will declare unto thee.

11. Shurippak,[65] a city which thou thyself knowest,

12. On [the bank] of the river Puratti (Euphrates) is situated,

13. That city was old and the gods [dwelling] within it—

14. Their hearts induced the great gods to make a wind-storm (𒅎𒆙𒈨, a-bu-bi),[66]

15. Their father Anu (𒀭𒄷𒆠𒐌),

16. Their counsellor, the warrior Enlil (𒀭𒆤𒐌),

17. Their messenger En-urta (𒀭𒌋𒁕𒈾)[and]

18. Their prince Ennugi (𒀭𒆤𒄀𒄀).

19. Nin-igi-azag, Ea, was with them [in council] and

20. reported their word to the house of reeds.

[First Speech of Ea to Uta-Napishtim who is sleeping in a reed hut]

21. O House of reeds, O House of reeds! O Wall, O Wall!

22. O House of reeds, hear! O Wall, understand!

23. O man of Shurippak,son of Ubara-Tutu (𒈗𒂷𒌋𒁕𒁕).

24. Throw down the house, build a ship,

25. Forsake wealth, seek after life,

---

[65] The site of this very ancient city is marked by the mounds of Fârah, near the Shaṭṭ al-Kâr, which is probably the old bed of the river Euphrates; many antiquities belonging to the earliest period of the rule of the Sumerians have been found there.

[66] Like the habûb of modern times, a sort of cyclone.

26. Abandon possessions, save thy life,

27. Carry grain of every kind into the ship.

28. The ship which thou shalt build,

29. The dimensions thereof shall be measured,

30. The breadth and the length thereof shall be the same.

31. ... the ocean, provide it with a roof."

[Uta-Napishtim's answer to Ea]

32. "I understood and I said unto Ea, my lord:

33. [I comprehend] my lord, that which thou hast ordered,

34. I will regard it with great reverence, and will perform it.

35. But what shall I say to the town, to the multitude, and to the elders?"

[Second Speech of Ea]

36. "Ea opened his mouth and spake

37. And said unto his servant, myself,

38. ... Thus shalt thou say unto them:

39. Ill-will hath the god Enlil formed against me,

40. Therefore I can no longer dwell in your city,

41. And never more will I turn my countenance upon the soil of Enlil.

42. I will descend into the ocean to dwell with my lord Ea.

43. But upon you he will rain riches:

44. A catch of birds, a catch of fish

45. ... an [abundant] harvest,

46. ... the prince (?) of the darkness

47. ... shall make a violent cyclone [to fall upon you]."

[The Building of the Ship]

48. As soon as [the dawn] broke...

[Lines 49–54 broken away.]

55. The weak [man] ... brought bitumen,

56. The strong [man] ... brought what was needed.

57. On the fifth day I decided upon its plan.

58. According to the plan its walls were 10 *Gar* (*i.e.* 120 cubits) high,

59. And the circuit of the roof thereof was equally 10 *Gar*.

60. I measured out the hull thereof and marked it out (?)

61. I covered (?) it six times.

62. Its exterior I divided into seven,

63. Its interior I divided into nine,

64. Water bolts I drove into the middle of it.

65. I provided a steering pole, and fixed what was needful for it,

66. Six *sar* of bitumen I poured over the inside wall,

67. Three *sar* of pitch I poured into the inside.

68. The men who bear loads brought three *sar* of oil,

69. Besides a *sar* of oil which the offering consumed,

70. And two *sar* of oil which the boatman hid.

71. I slaughtered oxen for the [work]people,

72. I slew sheep every day.

73. Beer, sesame wine, oil and wine

74. I made the people drink as if they were water from the river.

75. I celebrated a feast-day as if it had been New Year's Day.

76. I opened [a box of ointment], I laid my hands in unguent.

77. Before the sunset the ship was finished.

78. [Since] ... was difficult.

79. The shipbuilders brought the ... of the ship, above and below,

80. ... two-thirds of it.

[The Loading of the Ship]

81. With everything that I possessed I loaded it (*i.e.* the ship).

82. With everything that I possessed of silver I loaded it.

83. With everything that I possessed of gold I loaded it.

84. With all that I possessed of living grain I loaded it.

85. I made to go up into the ship all my family and kinsfolk,

86. The cattle of the field, the beasts of the field, all handicraftsmen I made them go up into it.

87. The god Shamash had appointed me a time (saying)

88. The Power of Darkness will at eventide make a rain-flood to fall;

89. Then enter into the ship and shut thy door.

90. The appointed time drew nigh;

91. The Power of Darkness made a rain-flood to fall at eventide.

92. I watched the coming of the [approaching] storm,

93. "When I saw it terror possessed me,

94. I went into the ship and shut my door.

95. To the pilot of the ship, Puzur-Bêl (or Puzur-Amurri 𒀭 𒇶𒂷 𒌨𒊩 𒋼 𒅀) the sailor

96. I committed the great house (*i.e.* ship), together with the contents thereof.

[The Abubu (Cyclone) and its effects Described]

97. As soon as the gleam of dawn shone in the sky

98. A black cloud from the foundation of heaven came up.

99. Inside it the god Adad (Rammânu) thundered,

100. The gods Nabû and Sharru (*i.e.* Marduk) went before,

101. Marching as messengers over high land and plain,

102. Irragal (Nergal) tore out the post of the ship,

103. En-urta (Ninib) went on, he made the storm to descend.

104. The Anunnaki[67] brandished their torches,

105. With their glare they lighted up the land.

---

[67] The star-gods of the southern sky.

106. The whirlwind (or, cyclone) of Adad swept up to heaven.

107. Every gleam of light was turned into darkness.

108. ...... the land ...... as if ...... had laid it waste.

109. A whole day long [the flood descended] ...

110. Swiftly it mounted up ..... [the water] reached to the mountains

111. [The water] attacked the people like a battle.

112. Brother saw not brother.

113. Men could not be known (or, recognized) in heaven.

114. The gods were terrified at the cyclone.

115. They betook themselves to flight and went up into the heaven of Anu.

116. The gods crouched like a dog and cowered by the wall.

117. The goddess Ishtar cried out like a woman in travail.

118. The Lady of the Gods lamented with a loud voice [saying]:

[Ishtar's Lament]

119. "Verily the former dispensation is turned into mud,

120. Because I commanded evil among the company of the gods.

121. When I commanded evil among the company of the gods,

122. I commanded battle for the destruction of my people.

123. Did I of myself bring forth my people

124. That they might fill the sea like little fishes?"

[Uta-Napishtim's Story continued]

125. The gods of the Anunnaki wailed with her.

126. The gods bowed themselves, and sat down, and wept.

127. Their lips were shut tight (in distress) ...

128. For six days and nights

129. The storm raged, and the cyclone overwhelmed the land.

[The Abating of the Storm]

130. When the seventh day approached the cyclone and the raging flood ceased:

131. —now it had fought like an army.

132. The sea became quiet and went down, and the cyclone and the rain-storm ceased.

133. I looked over the sea and a calm had come,

134. And all mankind were turned into mud,

135. The land had been laid flat like a terrace.

136. I opened the air-hole and the light fell upon my face,

137. I bowed myself, I sat down, I cried,

138. My tears poured down over my cheeks.

139. I looked over the quarters of the world—open sea!

140. After twelve days an island appeared.

141. The ship took its course to the land of Nisir (𒆜 𒌋 𒅖).

142. The mountain of Nisir held the ship, it let it not move.

143. The first day, the second day, the mountain of Nisir held the ship and let it not move.

144. The third day, the fourth day, the mountain of Nisir held the ship and let it not move.

145. The fifth day, the sixth day, the mountain of Nisir held the ship and let it not move.

146. When the seventh day had come

147. I brought out a dove and let her go free.

148. The dove flew away and [then] came back;

149. Because she had no place to alight on she came back.

150. I brought out a swallow and let her go free.

151. The swallow flew away and [then] came back;

152. Because she had no place to alight on she came back.

153. I brought out a raven and let her go free.

154. The raven flew away, she saw the sinking waters.

155. She ate, she pecked in the ground, she croaked, she came not back.

[Uta-Napishtim Leaves the Ship]

156. Then I brought out everything to the four winds and offered up a sacrifice;

157. I poured out a libation on the peak of the mountain.

158. Seven by seven I set out the vessels,

159. Under them I piled reeds, cedarwood and myrtle (?).

160. The gods smelt the savour,

161. The gods smelt the sweet savour.

162. The gods gathered together like flies over him that sacrificed.

[Speech of Ishtar, Lady of the Gods]

163. Now when the Lady of the Gods came nigh,

164. She lifted up the priceless jewels which Anu had made according to her desire, [saying]

165. "O ye gods here present, as I shall never forget the lapis-lazuli jewels of my neck

166. So shall I ever think about these days, and shall forget them nevermore!

167. Let the gods come to the offering,

168. But let not Enlil come to the offering,

169. Because he would not accept counsel and made the cyclone,

170. And delivered my people over to destruction."

[The Anger of Enlil (Bêl)]

171. Now when Enlil came nigh

172. He saw the ship; then was Enlil wroth

173. And he was filled with anger against the gods, the Igigi [saying]:[68]

174. "What kind of a being hath escaped with his life?

---

[68] The star-gods of the northern heaven.

175. He shall not remain alive, a man among the destruction!"

[Speech of En-Urta]

176. Then En-Urta opened his mouth and spake

177. And said unto the warrior Enlil (Bêl):

178. Who besides the god Ea can make a plan?

179. The god Ea knoweth everything.

180. He opened his mouth and spake

181. And said unto the warrior Enlil (Bêl),

182. O Prince among the gods, thou warrior,

183. How couldst thou, not accepting counsel, make a cyclone?

184. He who is sinful, on him lay his sin,

185. He who transgresseth, on him lay his transgression.

186. But be merciful that [everything] be not destroyed; be long-suffering that [man be not blotted out].

187. Instead of thy making a cyclone,

188. Would that a lion had come and diminished mankind.

189. Instead of thy making a cyclone

190. Would that a wolf had come and diminished mankind.

191. Instead of thy making a cyclone

192. Would that a famine had arisen and [laid waste] the land.

193. Instead of thy making a cyclone

194. Would that Urra (𒀭𒄑𒉈, the Plague god) had risen up and [laid waste] the land.

105

195. As for me I have not revealed the secret of the great gods.

196. I made Atra-hasis (ᴱᴱ! ᴱ⊦!! !!< ᴱ⊞<) to see a vision, and thus he heard the secret of the gods.

197. Now therefore counsel him with counsel."

[Ea deifies Uta-Napishtim and his Wife]

198. "Then the god Ea went up into the ship,

199. He seized me by the hand and brought me forth.

200. He brought forth my wife and made her to kneel by my side.

201. He turned our faces towards each other, he stood between us, he blessed us [saying],

202. Formerly Uta-Napishtim was a man merely,

203. But now let Uta-Napishtiin and his wife be like unto the gods, ourselves.

204. Uta-Napishtim shall dwell afar off, at the mouth of the rivers."

[Uta-Napishtim Ends his Story of the Deluge]

205. "And they took me away to a place afar off, and made me to dwell at the mouth of the rivers."

The contents of the remainder of the text on the Eleventh Tablet of the Gilgamish Series are described on p. 121.

The narrative of the life, exploits and travels of Gilgamish, king of Erech, filled Twelve Tablets which formed the Series called from the first three words of the First Tablet, *Sha Nagbu Imuru, i.e.,* "He who hath seen all things." The exact period of the reign of this king is unknown, but there is no doubt that he lived and ruled at Erech before the conquest of Mesopotamia by the Semites. According to a tablet from Niffar he was the fifth of a line of Sumerian rulers at Erech, and he reigned 126 years; his name is said to mean "The Fire-god is a commander."[70] The principal authorities for the Epic are the numerous fragments of the tablets that were found in the ruins of the Library of Nebo and the Royal Library of Ashur-bani-pal at Nineveh, and are now in the British Museum.[71] The contents of the Twelve Tablets may be briefly described thus:

The First Tablet

The opening lines describe the great knowledge and wisdom of Gilgamish, who saw everything, learned everything, understood everything, who probed to the bottom the hidden mysteries of wisdom, and who knew the history of everything that happened before the Deluge. He travelled far over sea and land, and performed mighty deeds, and then he cut upon a tablet of stone an account of all that he had done and suffered. He built the wall of Erech, founded the holy temple of E-Anna, and carried out other great architectural works. He was a semi-divine being, for his body was formed of the "flesh of the gods" 𒐀𒐀 𒀭 𒈠, and "Two-thirds of him were god, and one-third was man" 𒐉𒐉 𒐉𒐉 𒐉 𒀭 𒐉

---

[69] The name of Gilgamish was formerly read "Izdubar," "Gizdubar," or "Gishdubar." He is probably referred to as [GR: Gilgamos] in Aelian, De Natura Animalium, XII, 21 (ed. Didot, Paris, 1858, p. 210).

[70] Langdon, Epic of Gilgamish, pp. 207, 208.

[71] The greater number of these have been collected, grouped and published by Haupt, Das Babylonische Nimrodepos, Leipzig, 1884 and 1891; and see his work on the Twelfth Tablet in Beiträge zur Assyriologie, Vol. I, p. 49ff.

⟨𒐊𒈨𒐊 𒂖𒌍 𒌍𒐊𒐊 𒌋 𒅍 𒐊 𒅖 ᷄𒐊 (1. 51). The description of his person is lost. As Shepherd (*i.e.*, King) of Erech he forced the people to toil overmuch, and his demands reduced them to such a state of misery that they cried out to the gods and begged them to create some king who should control Gilgamish and give them deliverance from him. The gods hearkened to the prayer of the men of Erech, and they commanded the goddess Aruru to create a rival to Gilgamish. The goddess agreed to do their bidding, and having planned in her mind what manner of being she intended to make, she washed her hands, took a piece of clay and spat upon it, and made a male creature like the god Anu. His body was covered all over with hair. The hair of his head was long like that of a woman, and he wore clothing like that of Gira (or, Sumuggan), a goddess of vegetation, *i.e.*, he appeared to be clothed with leaves. He was different in every way from the people of the country, and his name was Enkidu (Eabani). He lived in the forests on the hills, ate herbs like the gazelle, drank with the wild cattle, and herded with the beasts of the field. He was mighty in stature, invincible in strength, and obtained complete mastery over all the creatures of the forests in which he lived.

One day a certain hunter went out to snare game, and he dug pit-traps and laid nets, and made his usual preparations for roping in his prey. But after doing this for three days he found that his pits were filled up and his nets smashed, and he saw Enkidu releasing the beasts that had been snared. The hunter was terrified at the sight of Enkidu, and went home hastily and told his father what he had seen and how badly he had fared. By his father's advice he went to Erech, and reported to Gilgamish what had happened. When Gilgamish heard his story he advised him to act upon a suggestion which the hunter's father had already made, namely that he should hire a harlot and take her out to the forest, so that Enkidu might be ensnared by the sight of her beauty, and take up his abode with her. The hunter accepted this advice, and having found a harlot to help him in removing Enkidu from the forests (thus enabling him to gain a living), he set out from Erech with her and in due course arrived at the forest where Enkidu lived, and sat down by the place where the beasts came to drink.

On the second day when the beasts came to drink and Enkidu was with them, the woman carried out the instructions which the hunter had given her, and when Enkidu saw her cast aside her veil, he left his beasts and came to her, and remained with her for six days and seven nights. At the end of this period he returned to the beasts with which he had lived on friendly terms, but as soon as the gazelle winded him they took to flight, and the wild cattle disappeared into the woods. When Enkidu saw the beasts forsake him his knees gave way, and he swooned from sheer shame; but when he came to himself he returned to the harlot. She spoke to him flattering words, and asked him why he wandered with the wild beasts in the desert, and then told him she wished to take him back with her to Erech, where Anu and Ishtar lived, and where the mighty Gilgamish reigned. Enkidu hearkened and finally went back with her to her city, where she described the wisdom, power and might of Gilgamish, and took steps to make Enkidu known to him. But before Enkidu arrived, Gilgamish had been warned of his existence and coming in two dreams which he related to his mother Ninsunna (⊣ ⟨⊨⟩ ⟨⊠⟩ ⊣⟨), and when he and Enkidu learned to know each other subsequently, these two mighty heroes became great friends.

The Second Tablet

When Enkidu came to Erech the habits of the people of the city were strange to him, but under the tuition of the harlot he learned to eat bread and to drink beer, and to wear clothes, and he anointed his body with unguents. He went out into the forests with his hunting implements and snared the gazelle and slew the panther, and obtained animals for sacrifice, and gained reputation as a mighty hunter and as a good shepherd. In due course he attracted the notice of Gilgamish, who did not, however, like his uncouth appearance and ways, but after a time, when the citizens of Erech praised him and admired his strong and vigorous stature, he made friends with him and rejoiced in him, and planned an expedition with him. Before they set out, Gilgamish wished to pay a visit to the goddess Ishkhara (⊣ ⟨⊨⟩ ⟨⊩⟩ ⟨⊨⟩), but Enkidu, fearing that the influence of the goddess would have a bad effect upon his friend, urged him to abandon the visit. This Gilgamish refused to do, and when Enkidu declared that by force he would prevent him going to the goddess, a violent quarrel broke out between the two heroes, and they appealed to arms. After a fierce fight Enkidu conquered Gilgamish, who apparently abandoned his visit to the goddess. The text of the Second Tablet is very much mutilated, and the authorities on the subject are not agreed as to the exact placing of the fragments. The above details are derived from a tablet at Philadelphia.[72]

The Third Tablet

The correct order of the fragments of this Tablet has not yet been ascertained, but among the contents of the first part of its text a lament by Enkidu that he was associated with the harlot seems to have had a place. Whether he had left the city of Erech and gone back to his native forest is not clear, but the god Shamash, having heard his cursing of the harlot, cried to him from heaven, saying, "Why, O Enkidu, dost thou curse the temple woman? She gave thee food to eat which was meet only for a god, she gave thee wine to drink which was meet only for a king, she arrayed thee in splendid apparel, and made thee to possess as thy friend the noble Gilgamish. And at present Gilgamish is thy bosom friend. He maketh thee to lie down on a large couch, and to sleep in a good, well-decked bed, and to occupy the chair of peace, the chair on the left-hand side. The princes of the earth kiss thy feet. He maketh the people of Erech to sigh for thee, and many folk to cry out for thee, and to serve thee. And for thy sake he putteth on coarse attire and arrayeth himself in the skin of the lion, and pursueth thee over the plain." When Enkidu heard these words his anxious heart had peace.

To the Third Tablet probably belongs the fragment in which Enkidu relates to Gilgamish a horrifying dream which he had had. In his dream it seemed to him that there were thunderings in heaven and quaking upon earth, and a being with an awful visage, and nails like all eagle's talons, gripped him and carried him off and forced him to go down into the dark abyss of the dread goddess, Irkalla. From this abode he who once "went in never came out, and he who travelled along that road never returned, he who dwelleth there is without light, the beings therein eat dust and feed upon mud; they are clad in feathers and have wings like birds, they see no light, and they live in the darkness of night." Here Enkidu saw in his dream creatures

---

[72] See Langdon, The Epic of Gilgamesh, Philadelphia, 1917.

who had been kings when they lived upon the earth, and shadowy beings offering roasted meat to Anu and Enlil, and cool drinks poured out from waterskins. In this House of Dust dwelt high priests, ministrants, the magician and the prophet, and the deities Etana, Sumukan, Eresh-kigal, Queen of the Earth, and Bêlitsêri, who registered the deeds done upon the earth.

When Gilgamish heard this dream, he brought out a table, and setting on it honey and butter placed it before Shamash.

The Fourth Tablet

Gilgamish then turned to Enkidu and invited him to go with him to the temple of Nin-Makh to see the servant of his mother, Ninsunna, in order to consult her as to the meaning of the dream. They went there, and Enkidu told his dream, and the wise woman offered up incense and asked Shamash why he had given to her son a heart which could never keep still. She next referred to the perilous expedition against the mighty King Khumbaba, which he had decided to undertake with Enkidu, and apparently hoped that the god would prevent her son from leaving Erech. But Gilgamish was determined to march against Khumbaba, and he and Enkidu set out without delay for the mountains where grew the cedars.

The Fifth Tablet

In due course the two heroes reached the forest of cedars, and they contemplated with awe their great height and their dense foliage. The cedars were under the special protection of Bêl, who had appointed to be their keeper Khumbaba, a being whose voice was like the roar of a storm, whose mouth was like that of the gods, and whose breath was like a gale of wind. When Enkidu saw how dense was the forest and how threatening, he tried to make Gilgamish turn back, but all his entreaties were in vain. As they were going through the forest to attack Khumbaba, Enkidu dreamed two or three dreams, and when he related them to Gilgamish, this hero

111

interpreted them as auguries of their success and the slaughter of Khumbaba. The fragmentary character of the text here makes it very difficult to find out exactly what steps the two heroes took to overcome Khumbaba, but there is no doubt that they did overcome him, and that they returned to Erech in triumph.

The Sixth Tablet

On his return to Erech, Gilgamish

1. Washed his armour, cleaned his weapons,

2. Dressed his hair and let it fall down on his back.

3. He cast off his dirty garments and put on clean ones

4. He arrayed himself in the [royal head-cloth], he bound on the fillet,

5. He put on his crown, he bound on the fillet.

6. Then the eyes of the Majesty of the goddess Ishtar lighted on the goodliness of Gilgamish [and she said],

7. "Go to, Gilgamish, thou shalt be my lover.

8. Give me thy [love]-fruit, give to me, I say.

9. Thou shalt be my man, I will be thy woman.

10. I will make to be harnessed for thee a chariot of lapis-lazuli and gold.

11. The wheels thereof shall be of gold and the horns of precious stones.

12. Thou shalt harness daily to it mighty horses.

13. Come into our house with the perfume of the cedar upon thee.

14. When thou enterest into our house

112

15. Those who sit upon thrones shall kiss thy feet.

16. Kings, lords and nobles shall bow their backs before thee.

17. The gifts of mountain and land they shall bring as tribute to thee.

18. Thy ... and thy sheep shall bring forth twins.

19. Baggage animals shall come laden with tribute.

20. The [horse] in thy chariot shall prance proudly,

21. There shall be none like unto the beast that is under thy yoke."

In answer to Ishtar's invitation Gilgamish makes a long speech, in which he reviews the calamities and misfortunes of those who have been unfortunate enough to become the lovers of the goddess. Her love is like a door that lets in wind and storm, a fortress that destroys the warriors inside it, an elephant that smashes his howdah, etc. He says, "What lover didst thou love for long? Which of thy shepherds flourished? Come now, I will describe the calamity [that goeth with thee]." He refers to Tammuz, the lover of her youth, for whom year by year she arranges wailing commemorations. Every creature that falls under her sway suffers mutilation or death, the bird's wings are broken, the lion is destroyed, the horse is driven to death with whip and spur; and his speech concludes with the words: "Dost thou love me, and wouldst thou treat me as thou didst them?"

Extract from the text of the Sixth Tablet of the Gilgamish Series (lines 50–70), containing a part of the speech which Gilgamish addressed to Ishtar in answer to her overtures to him. He reviles the goddess and reminds her of the death of Tammuz, and the sufferings of all the creatures that have been unfortunate enough to enter her service. From Rawlinson, Cuneiform Inscriptions Western Asia, Vol. IV, Plate 41, col. 2. (K. 2589.)

When Ishtar heard these words she was filled with rage, and she went up to heaven and complained to Anu, her father, and Antu, her mother, that Gilgamish had cursed her and revealed all her iniquitous deeds and actions. She followed up her complaint with the request that Anu should create a mighty bull of heaven to destroy Gilgamish, and she threatened her father that if he did not grant her request she would do works of destruction, presumably in the world. Anu created the fire-breathing (?) bull of heaven and sent him to the city of Erech, where he destroyed large numbers of the people. At length Enkidu and Gilgamish determined to go forth and slay the bull. When they came to the place where he was, Enkidu seized him by the tail, and Gilgamish delivered deadly blows between his neck and his horns, and together they killed, him. As soon as Ishtar heard of the death of the bull she rushed out on the battlements of the walls of Erech and cursed Gilgamish for destroying her bull. When Enkidu heard what Ishtar said, he went and tore off a portion of the bull's flesh from his right side, and threw it at the goddess, saying, "Could I but fight with thee I would serve thee as I have served him! I would twine his entrails about thee." Then Ishtar gathered together all her temple women and harlots, and with them made lamentation over the portion of the bull which Enkidu had thrown at her.

And Gilgamish called together the artisans of Erech who came and marvelled at the size of the bull's horns, for their bulk was equal to 30 minas of lapis-lazuli, and their thickness to the length of two fingers, and they could contain six *Kur* measures of oil. Then Gilgamish took them to the temple of the god Lugalbanda and hung them up there on the throne of his majesty, and having made his offering he and Enkidu went to the Euphrates and washed their hands, and walked back to the market-place of Erech. As they went through the streets of the city the people thronged about them to get a sight of their faces. When Gilgamish asked:

> "Who is splendid among men?
> Who is glorious among heroes?"

these questions were answered by the women of the palace who cried:

> "Gilgamish is splendid among men.
> Gilgamish is glorious among heroes."

When Gilgamish entered his palace he ordered a great festival to be kept, and his guests were provided by him with beds to sleep on. On the night of the festival Enkidu had a dream, and he rose up and related it to Gilgamish.

The Seventh Tablet

About the contents of the Seventh Tablet there is considerable doubt, and the authorities differ in their opinions about them. A large number of lines of text are wanting at the beginning of the Tablet, but it is very probable that they contained a description of Enkidu's dream. This may have been followed by an interpretation of the dream, either by Gilgamish or some one else, but whether this be so or not, it seems tolerably certain that the dream portended disaster for Enkidu. A fragment, which seems to belong to this Tablet beyond doubt, describes the sickness and death of Enkidu. The cause of his sickness is unknown, and the fragment merely states that he took to his bed and lay there for ten days, when his illness took a turn for the worse, and on the twelfth day he died. He may have died of wounds received in some fight, but it is more probable that he succumbed to an attack of Mesopotamian fever. When Gilgamish was told that his brave friend and companion in many fights was dead, he could not believe it, and he thought that he must be asleep, but when he found that death had really carried off Enkidu, he broke out into the lament which formed the beginning of the text of the next Tablet.

The Eighth Tablet

In this lament he calls Enkidu his brave friend and the "panther of the desert," and refers to their hunts in the mountains, and to their slaughter of the bull of heaven, and to the overthrow of Khumbaba in the forest of cedar, and then he asks him:

"What kind of sleep is this which hath laid hold upon thee?
"Thou starest out blankly (?) and hearest me not!"

But Enkidu moved not, and when Gilgamish touched his breast his heart was still. Then laying a covering over him oas carefully as if he had been his bride, he turned away from the dead body and in his grief roared like a raging lion and like a lioness robbed of her whelps.

The Ninth Tablet

In bitter grief Gilgamish wandered about the country uttering lamentations for his beloved companion, Enkidu. As he went about he thought to himself,

"I myself shall die, and shall not I then be as Enkidu?
"Sorrow hath entered into my soul,
"Because of the fear of death which hath got hold of me do I wander over the country."

His fervent desire was to escape from death, and remembering that his ancestor Uta-Napishtim, the son of Ubara-Tutu, had become deified and immortal, Gilgamish determined to set out for the place where he lived in order to obtain from him the secret of immortality. Where Uta-Napishtim lived was unknown to Gilgamish, but he seems to have made up his mind that he would have to face danger in reaching the place, for he says, "I will set out and travel quickly. I shall reach the defiles in the mountains by night, and if I see lions, and am terrified at them, I shall lift up my head and appeal to the goddess Sin, and to Ishtar, the Lady of the Gods, who is wont to hearken to my prayers." After Gilgamish set out to go to the west he was attacked either by men or animals, but he overcame them and went on until he arrived at Mount Mashu, where it would seem the sun was thought both to rise and to set. The approach to this mountain was guarded by Scorpion-men, whose aspect was so terrible that the mere sight of it was sufficient to kill the mortal who beheld them; even the mountains collapsed under the glance of their eyes. When Gilgamish saw the Scorpion-men he was smitten with fear, and under the influence of his terror the colour of his face changed; but he plucked up courage and bowed to them humbly. Then a Scorpion-man cried out to his wife, saying, "The body of him that cometh to us is the flesh of the gods," and she replied, "Two-thirds of him is god, and the other third is man." The Scorpion-man then received Gilgamish kindly, and warned him that the way which he was about to travel was full of danger and difficulty. Gilgamish told him that he was in search of his ancestor, Uta-Napishtim, who had been deified and made immortal by the gods, and that it was his intention to go to him to learn the secret of immortality. The Scorpion-man in answer told him that it was impossible for him to continue his journey through that country, for no man had ever succeeded in passing through the dark region of that mountain, which required twelve double-hours to traverse. Nothing dismayed, Gilgamish set out on the road through the mountains, and the darkness increased in density every hour, but he struggled on, and at the end of the twelfth hour he arrived at a region where there was bright daylight, and he entered a lovely garden, filled with trees loaded with luscious fruits, and he saw the "tree of the gods."

The Tenth Tablet

In the region to which Gilgamish had come stood the palace or fortress of the goddess Siduri-Sabîtu, and to this he directed his steps with the view of obtaining help to continue his journey. The goddess wore a girdle and sat upon a throne by the side of the sea, and when she saw him coming towards her palace, travel-stained and clad in the ragged skin of some animal, she thought that he might prove an undesirable visitor and so ordered the door of her palace to be closed against him. But Gilgamish managed to obtain speech with her, and having asked her what ailed her, and why she had closed her door, he threatened to smash the bolt and break down the door. In answer Siduri-Sabitu said to him:—

33. "Why are thy cheeks wasted? Thy face is bowed down,

34. "Thine heart is sad, thy form is dejected.

35. "Why is there lamentation in thy heart?"

And she went on to tell him that he had the appearance of one who had travelled far, that he was a painful sight to look upon, that his face was burnt, and finally seems to have suggested that he was a runaway trying to escape trom the country. To this Gilgamish replied:

39. "Why should not my cheeks be wasted, my face bowed down,

40. "My heart sad, my form dejected?"

And then he told the goddess that his ill-looks and miserable appearance were due to the fact that death had carried off his dear friend Enkidu, the "panther of the desert," who had traversed the mountains with him and had helped him to overcome Khumbaba in the cedar forest, and to slay the bull of heaven, Enkidu his dear friend who had fought with lions and killed them, and who had been with him in all his difficulties; and, he added, "I wept over him for six days and nights ... before I would let him be buried." Continuing his narrative, Gilgamish said to Sabîtu-Siduri:

57. "I was horribly afraid....

58. "I was afraid of death, and therefore I fled through the country. The fate of my friend lieth heavily upon me,

59. "Therefore am I travelling on a long journey through the country.

"The fate of my friend lieth heavily upon me,

60. "Therefore am I travelling on a long journey through the country.

61. "How is it possible for me to keep silence about it?

How is it possible for me to cry out [the story of] it?

62. "My friend whom I loved hath become like the dust.

"Enkidu, my friend whom I loved hath become like the dust.

63. "Shall not I myself also be obliged to lay me down

64. "And never again rise up to all eternity?"

65. Gilgamish [continued] to speak unto Sabîtu [saying]:

66. "[O] Sabîtu, which is the way to Uta-Napishtim?

67. "What is the description thereof? Give me, give me the description thereof.

68. "If it be possible I will cross the sea,

69. "If it be impossible I will travel by land."

70. Then Sabîtu answered and said unto Gilgamish:

71. "There is no passage most assuredly, O Gilgamish.

72. "And no one, from the earliest times, hath been able to cross the sea.

73. "The hero Shamash (the Sun-god) hath indeed crossed the sea, but who besides him could do so?

74. "The passage is hard, and the way is difficult.

75. "And the Waters of Death which block the other end of it are deep.

76. "How then, Gilgamish, wilt thou be able to cross the sea?

77. "When thou arrivest at the Waters of Death what wilt thou do?"

Sabîtu then told Gilgamish that Ur-Shanabi, the boatman of Uta-Napishtim, was in the place, and that he should see him, and added:

81. "If it be possible cross with him, and if it be impossible come back."

Gilgamish left the goddess and succeeded in finding Ur-Shanabi, the boatman, who addressed to him words similar to those of Sabîtu quoted above. Gilgamish answered him as he had answered Sabîtu, and then asked him for news about the road to Uta-Napishtim. In reply Ur-Shanabi told him to take his axe and to go down into the forest and cut a number of poles 60 cubits long; Gilgamish did so, and when he returned with them he went up into the boat with Ur-Shanabi, and they made a voyage of one month and fifteen days; on the third day they reached the [limit of the] Waters of Death, which Ur-Shanabi told Gilgamish not to touch with his hand. Meanwhile, Uta-Napishtim had seen the boat coming and, as something in its appearance seemed strange to him, he went down to the shore to see who the newcomers were. When he saw Gilgamish he asked him the same questions that Sabîtu and Ur-Shanabi had asked him, and Gilgamish answered as he had answered them, and then went on to tell him the reason for his coming. He said that he had determined to go to visit Uta-Napishtim, the remote, and had therefore journeyed far and that in the course of his travels he had passed over difficult mountains and crossed the sea. He had not succeeded in entering the house of Sabîtu, for she had caused him to be driven from her door on account of his dirty, ragged, and travel-stained apparel. He had eaten birds and beasts of many kinds, the lion, the panther, the jackal, the antelope, mountain goat, etc., and, apparently, had dressed himself in their skins.

A break in the text makes it impossible to give the opening lines of Uta-Napishtim's reply, but he mentions the father and mother of Gilgamish, and in the last twenty lines of the Tenth Tablet he warns Gilgamish that on earth there is nothing permanent, that Mammitum, the arranger of destinies, has settled the question of the death and life of man with the Anunnaki, and that none may find out the day of his death or escape from death.

The Eleventh Tablet

The story of the Deluge as told by Uta-Napishtim to Gilgamish has already been given on pp. 31–40, and we therefore pass on to the remaining contents of this Tablet. When Uta-Napishtim had finished the story of the Deluge, he said to Gilgamish, "Now as touching thyself; which of the gods will gather thee to himself so that thou mayest find the life which thou seekest? Come now, do not lay thyself down to sleep for six days and seven nights." But in spite of this admonition as soon as Gilgamish had sat down, drowsiness overpowered him and he fell fast asleep. Uta-Napishtim, seeing that even the mighty hero Gilgamish could not resist falling asleep, with some amusement drew the attention of his wife to the fact, but she felt sorry for the tired man, and suggested that he should take steps to help him to return to his home. In reply Uta-Napishtim told her to bake bread for him and she did so, and each day for six days she carried a loaf to the ship and laid it on the deck where Gilgamish lay sleeping. On the seventh day when she took the loaf Uta-Napishtim

121

touched Gilgamish, and the hero woke up with a start, and admitted that he had been overcome with sleep, and made incapable of movement thereby.

Still vexed with the thought of death and filled with anxiety to escape from it, Gilgamish asked his host what he should do and where he should go to effect his object. By Uta-Napishtim's advice, he made an agreement with Ur-Shanabi the boatman, and prepared to re-cross the sea on his way home. But before he set out on his way Uta-Napishtim told him of the existence of a plant which grew at the bottom of the sea, and apparently led Gilgamish to believe that the possession of it would confer upon him immortality. Thereupon Gilgamish tied heavy stones [to his feet], and let himself down into the sea through an opening in the floor of the boat. When he reached the bottom of the sea, he saw the plant and plucked it, and ascended into the boat with it. Showing it to Ur-Shanabi, he told him that it was a most marvellous plant, and that it would enable a man to obtain his heart's desire. Its name was "Shîbu issahir amelu," 𒀭 𒂊 𒆬 𒂍 𒅔 𒂊𒇻 𒂗, i.e., "The old man becometh young [again]," and Gilgamish declared that he would "eat of it in order to recover his lost youth," and that he would take it home to his fortified city of Erech. Misfortune, however, dogged his steps, and the plant never reached Erech, for whilst Gilgamish and Ur-Shanabi were on their way back to Erech they passed a pool the water of which was very cold, and Gilgamish dived into it and took a bath. Whilst there a serpent discovered the whereabouts of the plant through its smell and swallowed it. When Gilgamish saw what had happened he cursed aloud, and sat down and wept, and the tears coursed down his cheeks as he lamented over the waste of his toil, and the vain expenditure of his heart's blood, and his failure to do any good for himself. Disheartened and weary he struggled on his way with his friend, and at length they arrived at the fortified city of Erech.73 Then Gilgamish told Ur-Shanabi to jump up on the

---

73 The city of Erech was the second of the four cities which, according to Genesis x, 10, were founded by Nimrod, the son of Cush, the "mighty hunter before the Lord. And the beginning of his kingdom was Babel, and Erech and Accad, and Calneh, in the land of Shinar." The Sumerians and Babylonians called the city "Uruk Ki" ; the first sign means "dwelling" or "habitation," and the second "land, country," etc., and we may regard it as the "inhabited country," par excellence, of Lower Babylonia at a very early period. The site of Erech is well-known, and is marked by the vast ruins which the Arabs call "Warkah," or Al-Warkah. These lie in 31° 19′ N. Lat. and 45° 40′ E. Long., and are about four miles from the Euphrates, on the

wall and examine the bricks from the foundations to the battlements, and see if the plans which he had made concerning them had been carried out during his absence.

The Twelfth Tablet

The text of the Twelfth Tablet is very fragmentary, and contains large gaps, but it seems certain that Gilgamish did not abandon his hope of finding the secret of immortality. He had failed to find it upon earth, and he made arrangements with the view of trying to find it in the kingdom of the dead. The priests whom he consulted described to him the conditions under which he might hope to enter the Underworld, but he was unable to fulfil the obligations which they laid upon him, and he could not go there. Gilgamish then thought that if he could have a conversation with Enkidu, his dead friend, he might learn from him what he wanted to know. He

---

left or east bank of the river. Sir W. K. Loftus carried out excavations on the site in 1849–52, and says that the external walls nof sun-dried brick enclosing the main portion of the ruins form an irregular circle five and a half miles in circumference; in places they are from 40 to 50 feet in height, and they seem to have been about 20 feet thick. The turrets on the wall were semi-oval in shape, and about 50 feet apart. The principal ruin is that of the Ziggurat, or temple tower, which in 1850 was 100 feet high and 200 feet square. Loftus calls it "Buwáríya," i.e., "reed mats," because reed mats were used in its construction, but bûrîyah, "rush mat," is a Persian not Arabic word, and the name is more probably connected with the Arabic "Bawâr," i.e., "ruin" "place of death," etc. This tower stood in a courtyard which was 350 feet long and 270 feet wide. The next large ruin is that which is called "Waswas" (plur. "Wasâwis"), i.e., "large stone" The "Waswas" referred to was probably the block of columnar basalt which Loftus and Mr. T. K. Lynch found projecting through the soil; on it was sculptured the figure of a warrior, and the stone itself was regarded as a talisman by the natives. This ruin is 246 feet long, 174 feet wide and 80 feet high. On three sides of it are terraces of different elevations, but the south-west side presents a perpendicular façade, at one place 23 feet in height. For further details see Loftus, Chaldea and Susiana, London, 1857, p. 159 ff. Portions of the ruins of Warkah were excavated by the German archaeologists in 1914, and large "finds" of tablets and other antiquities are said to have been made.

appealed to Bêl and asked him to raise up the spirit of Enkidu for him, but Bêl made no answer; he then appealed to Sin, and this god also made no answer. He next appealed to Ea, who, taking pity on him, ordered the warrior god Nergal to produce the spirit of Enkidu, and this god opened a hole in the ground through which the spirit of Enkidu passed up into this world "like a breath of wind." Gilgamish began to ask the spirit of Enkidu questions, but gained very little information or satisfaction. The last lines of the tablet seem to say that the spirit of the unburied man reposeth not in the earth, and that the spirit of the friendless man wandereth about the streets eating the remains of food which are cast out from the cooking pots.

E. A. Wallis Budge

Department of Egyptian and Assyrian Antiquities, British Museum,

July 24th, 1920

PLATES

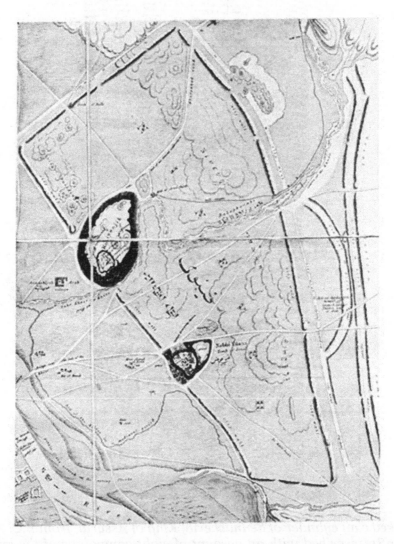

Plan of the ruins of the walls, temples and palaces of Nineveh, showing the course of the River Khausur, and the great protective ditches outside the eastern wall. The southern mound (Nabi Yûnis) contains the ruins of palaces, etc., built by Sargon II, Sennacherib and Esarhaddon, and the northern mound (Kuyûnjik) the Palaces and Library of Ashur-bani-pal, the Library of Nebo, etc. From the drawing made by the late Commander Felix Jones, I.N.

Baked clay cylinder of Sennacherib, King of Assyria, from B.C. 705 to 681, inscribed with an account of eight campaigns of the king, including the capture and sack of Babylon, the invasion of Palestine, and the siege of Jerusalem; it is dated in the eponymy of Bel-imurani, i.e., B.C. 691. B.M. No. 91,032. This cylinder was found among the ruins of a palace of Sennacherib under the mound of Nabi Yûnis, and was bought by Colonel J. Taylor, Consul-General of Baghdâd in 1830, from whose representatives it was bought by the Trustees of the British Museum in 1855.

Baked clay six-sided cylinder, inscribed with the Annals of Esarhaddon, King of Assyria from B.C. 681–668. B.M. No. 91,028. This cylinder was found in the ruins of the palace of Esarhaddon, under the mound of Nabi Yûnis, and had been "used as a candlestick by a respectable Turcoman family living in the village on the mound near the tomb of the prophet [Jonah]." The grease marks from the candles are still visible on it. It was acquired by Sir Henry Layard and presented by him to the British Museum in 1848.

Specimens of Tablets from Nineveh.

1. *Astrological report concerning divinations of the Moon.*
2. *Astrological report concerning the Moon and Mercury.*
3. *Prayers of Ashur-bani-pal to Nebo.*

Specimens of Tablets from Nineveh.

1. Part of a mythological legend concerning early Babylonian rulers.
2. Assyrian letter.
3 and 4. Letter and envelope from Ashur-ritsûa to an official.

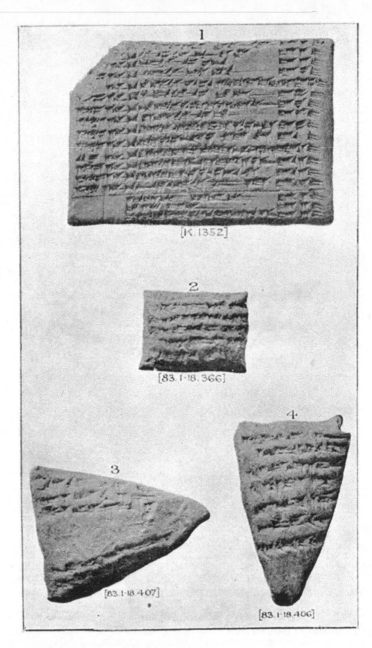

Specimens of Tablets from Nineveh.

1. Catologue of Omen tablets, giving the first line of each.
2. Contract tablet, written B.C. 675.
3. Contract tablet, with the impression of a seal; written B.C. 693.
4. Contract tablet, written B.C. 686.

130

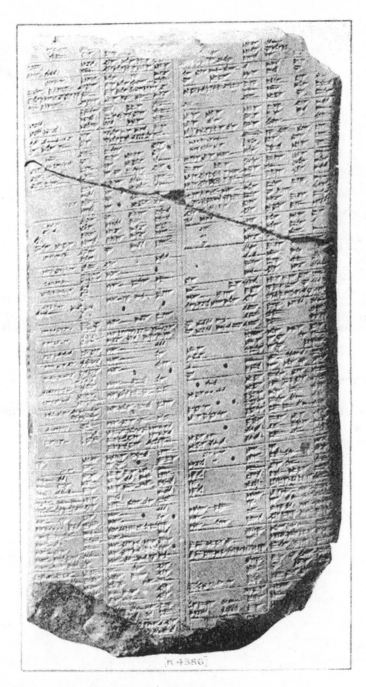

Specimen of Tablets from Nineveh.

Explanatory List of Words with glosses.

131

Specimens of Tablets from Nineveh.

1. Label, inscribed with the title of a series of strological forecasts.
2. Label, inscribed with the title of a series of omens.
3. Part of a text containing grammatical paradigms.

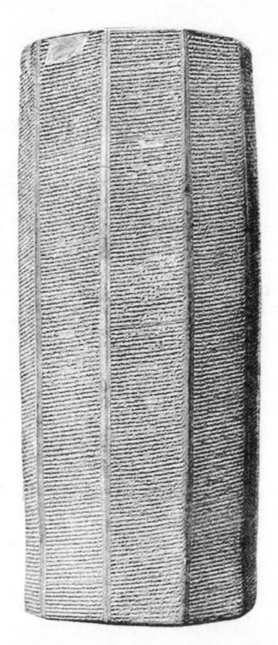

Baked clay ten-sided cylinder inscribed with a description of the most important events of the reign of Ashur-bani-pal, king of Assyria, B.C. 668–626, and an account of the building operations which he carried on in Nineveh. B.M. No. 91,026. This cylinder was discovered in a chamber in one of the main walls of the palace of Ashur-bani-pal at Nineveh by Mr. Hormuzd Rassam in 1878.

Scene on bas-relief from a chamber in the palace of Ashur-bani-pal at Nineveh, in which the king is represented standing before a table of offerings and a divine symbol and pouring out a libation over a group of dead lions. Assyrian Saloon, No. 118.

[K. 47]

Tablet from the Temple of Nebo with Colophon.

Astrological Omens concerning cities.

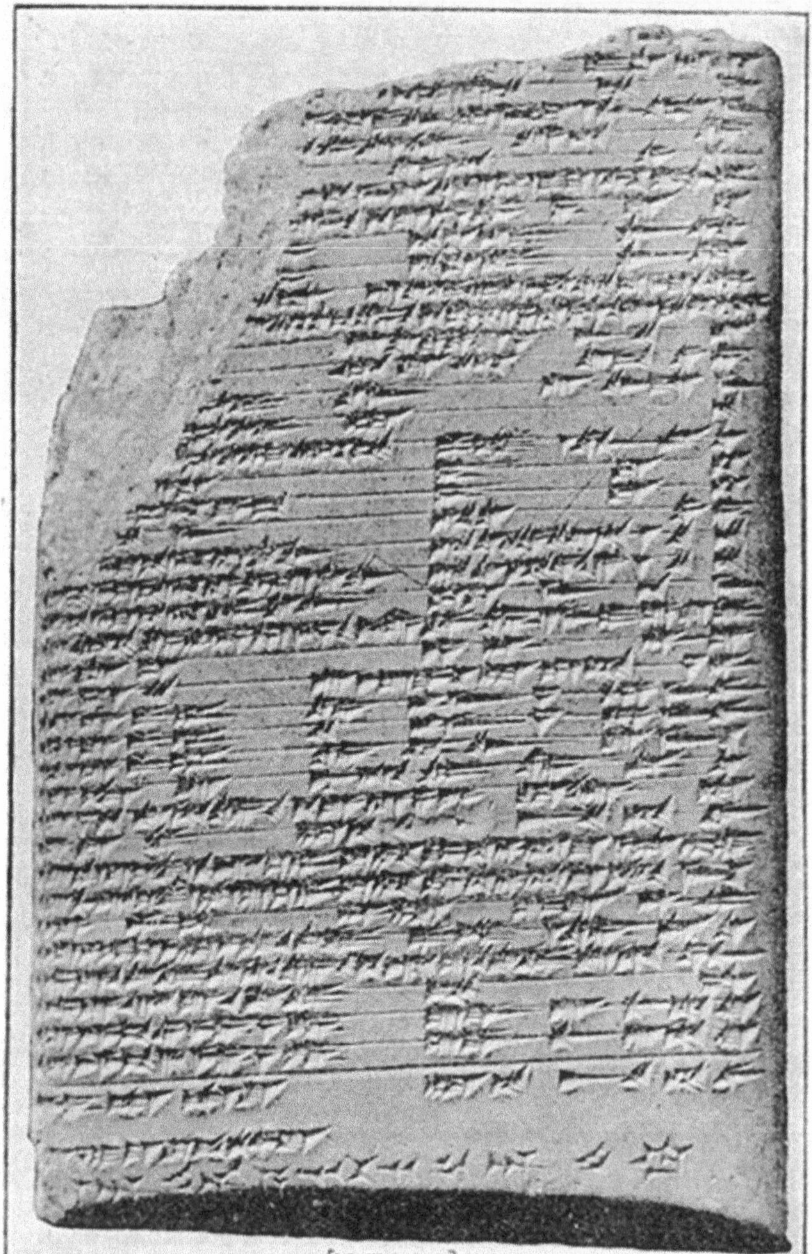

[K 7000]

Tablet from the Temple of Nebo with Colophon.

Forecasts which formed the Fourth Tablet of the Series .

The Eleventh Tablet of the Gilgamish Series containing the Story of the Deluge as told to Gilgamish by his deified ancestor Uta-Napishtim, an antediluvian king of Erech. A portion of one end of the tablets was vitrified when Ashur-bani-pal's palace and the Librrary of Nebo were destroyed by fire. From the Library of the Temple of Nebo. Size, seven-eighths of the original.
K. 3321 + S. 1881

Portion of another copy of the Story of the Deluge, from a tablet which probably belonged to the Palace of Ashur-bani-pal at Nineveh. Photograph one-seventh larger than the original. K. 3375